ISBN 978-1-330-46163-1
PIBN 10011138

1 MONTH OF
FREE
READING

at

www.ForgottenBooks.com

By purchasing this book you are eligible for one month membership to ForgottenBooks.com, giving you unlimited access to our entire collection of over 700,000 titles via our web site and mobile apps.

To claim your free month visit:

www.forgottenbooks.com/free11138

English
Français
Deutsche
Italiano
Español
Português

www.forgottenbooks.com

Mythology Photography **Fiction**
Fishing Christianity **Art** Cooking
Essays Buddhism Freemasonry
Medicine **Biology** Music **Ancient
Egypt** Evolution Carpentry Physics
Dance Geology **Mathematics** Fitness
Shakespeare **Folklore** Yoga Marketing
Confidence Immortality Biographies
Poetry **Psychology** Witchcraft
Electronics Chemistry History **Law**
Accounting **Philosophy** Anthropology
Alchemy Drama Quantum Mechanics
Atheism Sexual Health **Ancient History**
Entrepreneurship Languages Sport
Paleontology Needlework Islam
Metaphysics Investment Archaeology
Parenting Statistics Criminology
Motivational

The LAW *of* MIND *in* ACTION

Daily Lessons and Treatments
in Mental and Spiritual Science

by

FENWICKE L. HOLMES

Author of "Being and Becoming," the "Unfailing Formula,"
"How to Realize the Presence," etc; Associate Editor of the
"Uplift"; Founder (with E. S. Holmes) of The Southern
California Metaphysical Institute.

NEW YORK
ROBERT M. McBRIDE & CO.
1919

BF639
H65

Printed in the United States of America.

PUBLISHED MAY, 1919.

CONTENTS

PART II.

TREATMENTS OR REALIZATIONS.

LESSON

Metaphysical Institute Realization

GOD is Creative Spirit, everywhere present, eternally here. In Him is all life, intelligence, goodness, holiness and truth. He knows no want. He suffers no pain. He is unlimited in time, space and circumstance.

Man, child of God, is divine spirit, shares His resources, lives, moves and has his being in God as an infinite sea. "There is one God and Father of all, who is over all, through all, and in all."

As His child, therefore, I am pure spirit, free from ills of body, mind and soul. In pure spirit I live, move and have my being. I am perfect, even as my Father in heaven is perfect. The breath which I breathe, is the breath of the Spirit. The food which I eat is the gift of the Spirit and it fills me with the strength of the Spirit. The consciousness of the Perfect Spirit is mine, and I know it and feel it flowing through my whole being, bringing with it strength, power, and perfect peace. The Spirit of the Lord is upon me, and I feel His presence all around me, in me, and through me. I am free from all sickness, worry and fear. Perfect love casts out all fear from me and I am free. Health, hope, peace, life, love, truth, and plenty are mine. These I claim from God. These in the name of Christ I **Now** receive. I render thanks for the perfect gift.

THERE is a law of healing so plain that even a child can understand it, so fundamental that the ablest mind has never yet thought through all the facts and phenomena of life that rest upon it. It is the purpose of this book to make this law plain

The greatest power in the world is the power of thought, for it is Creative Mind in action. Nothing exists that did not first exist in thought from the first sun that blazed only in the Mind of the Creator, to the last doll-dress fashioned by a childish hand. Science supports the fact that the first movement in nature can have come only from the application of an immaterial force or Will to the primary etheric particles otherwise in a perfect state of equilibrium. It must leave to metaphysics not only an explanation of the Will that moves but also the substance that is moved. This, then, it is the province of this book to show with all that it entails. Since an act of Will is an act of mind, we concern ourselves with the activity of a Creative Mind. Again since Mind acts creatively, there is a *way* in which it acts. We must also, therefore, teach the *way*. It is to teach this *way* that the Bible was written, that Jesus lived and taught. This way has been known for many centuries but has always been taught in terms of the understanding of the day in which the teacher lived. The Great Metaphysician taught largely in parables and oriental figures of speech. But He taught "the Way" and his followers were called the People of the Way.

The *"way" is the law and today the understanding of it as law enables us to put, in a few simple statements which all can understand, the principles of the law, which, if learned and used, will enable anyone to control the conditions of his body, mind, and environment. Anyone can learn how to use it.*

It is clear to us that it is natural to use the power of Mind and that the greatest happiness results from its exercise.

Mind is so constituted that it *must* act, it must express that which it feels itself to be. All nature points to the fact that wherever action ceases, death, or negation, begins. Mind is the very spirit of the life in nature and therefore is eternally active. Yet it is also infinite repose for it is that out of which all activity springs and by which it is sustained. In this book we are not dealing so much with that great *potential* of activity which we call being as with the *law* by which it acts. We are concerned not so much with the contemplation of the Life, Love, and Wisdom, which is God or Being, as with the *way* Spirit manifests. How life becomes health, how love becomes happiness, and how wisdom becomes wealth, we desire to know. As these are all qualities of mind, and in their pure state are undifferentiated into form, we realize that when they begin to pass out into individual expression, it must be by the process of thinking. That is the only way mind can act. So that the Creative process is simply Mind in action, or Mind thinking its Life, Love and Wisdom into form. Mind in action is always creative, but it is also thought. Thought acts in Mind to create. Or mind first produces thought and then reacts to it to become that which it has thought. This is the whole law of creation. Mind creates what it thinks. The many forms pass out of the one Mind, but each form has a corresponding thought which produces and sustains it.

Mind in action is, therefore, also the law. We call it the law of cause and effect. Law is the principle on which mind works. For every primary cause is in the mind and the effect is simply the form which thought has taken. Thought is first cause, in any created series, and form is effect.

Thought acts upon mind to produce things. Since things are made out of mind, they are simply thought in form, but they maintain form and reality only so long as they are sustained by the thought.

The Law, therefore, may be defined as mind in action producing the many out of the one by the power of thought, and this book is written to furnish a daily meditation on the highest of all themes—man's control of his own body, happiness, circumstances and environment by the thoughts which he thinks. The knowledge and use of thought and the law of mind in action is the knowledge of which Jesus spoke when he said, "Ye shall know the truth and the truth shall make you free." May these pages free many to the glorious wisdom of Mind in Action.

FENWICKE L. HOLMES.

December 30, 1918.

METHOD OF READING AND STUDY OF "THE LAW OF MIND IN ACTION."

THIS book is written to teach the one simple law of mind—The Law—which anyone can understand and use, and which if used will give freedom, joy, health, supply, and peace to the one who uses it. This is a big claim, but it is supported by the Bible, by the Great Teacher, and by the experience of thousands now living. Everything in this book is based on the Law outlined in Lesson II and the student is requested to read each chapter and then ask himself, "How does this illustrate the Law? Is it true to the Law?" Always do this and you will soon know the Law for yourself and can use it and teach it to others. Thus you will become a master of life.

This book is designed also to stimulate your own thinking and investigation. It is not expected that the beginner will grasp the full significance of all the principles at one reading. It is for meditation. Read and **Think**. Make a study of life, books, newspapers, men and events with reference to this Law and you will find thousands of illustrations of it. When you can reduce all the phenomena of life to this Law, you have become a great philosopher.

If you are entering on this kind of study for the first time, do not allow offense at some one statement

6

to discourage your further reading. Perhaps you have not yet understood it in the way it was meant. Perhaps it is so new a view that you do not want to believe it yet. Go on reading and studying and make your own decisions. As Paul says, "Prove all things, hold fast that which is good." Even if you should never accept it all, you can still get help, and find health and peace.

A close study of these lessons will reveal to the student that they are not brought together by a chance arrangement but are consecutive. First, we have the meaning and definition of metaphysics and the Law. Then the general principles of its application are given. These in turn are followed by the philosophy of metaphysics. Fourth, we have an explanation of the reason for certain mental attitudes and how the Law applies; this is a study in cause and effect. Fifth, we consider the Law as related to the Absolute and the Personal Spirit. Sixth, and finally, we devote our attention to specific methods and treatments. These should all be studied systematically.

Too much emphasis cannot be laid on the necessity of systematic study. A mere smattering of metaphysics will never satisfy the demands of the day nor the inner requirements of the Law. We have a great body of truth. The world is anxious to know *why* we believe and teach what we do. No science in the world, no philosophy is more complete or comprehensive. We must learn it so completely that we can

teach it with the utmost simplicity as Jesus taught it.
Do not therefore go jumping about in your study.
A good principle of study is to read the book clear
through once if you wish to get a general view of
the principles so that you may know just about what
goal you are driving toward; after that *confine yourself each day to one lesson and know it.*   **Think**
more than you read.   Masterful study puts more between the lines than it takes from the lines.   This
is to stimulate your *own* thinking.   Thus you will
become a master teacher of life.

The word "treatment" as used in this book is a
synonym for realization or perception.   It is useless
to quarrel with language.   It *is* and there's an end
on't.   The word treatment has become sufficiently
popularized to mean to the general public what the
teacher of the absolute means by some other favorite
term, and it is safe to predicate that this term will
be supported by future as well as present usage.

In time the student will arrive at that point of consciousness where he will not need the formulated
treatment.   He will then form his own statement.
Ultimately he will be able to "speak the word only"
and it will be done unto him even as he thinks.   The
advanced metaphysician heals entirely by the word;
he reaches the point where he actually does perceive
the truth that is to make him free.

LESSON I.

METAPHYSICS—WHAT IT IS AND DOES.

THE word metaphysics, as its composition indicates, denotes something above the physical, "meta," meaning "over," and "physics" referring to forms of matter. So that to work upon the metaphysical plane means to employ laws that transcend physical means or agencies. It is, then, to push our way back of the thing that we see, which we call "the manifestation," until we find the cause of the manifestation. It is the search for the Ultimate Cause and the law by which the Spirit creates a world, and brings material objects and physical life into manifestation.

Our study of applied metaphysics is designed to make clear these facts: In the beginning there is only Mind or Spirit. Whatever is made, therefore, must be made out of Mind. Mind can act only by thinking; therefore it is thought that takes the substance called mind and moulds it into form. God makes a world out of himself. As everything in the cosmos starts in thought and manifests in form, creation is the process by which the activity takes place. We may call it evolution or we may call it law. By law we mean the method Spirit follows in making things. This is the law of cause and effect whether it be in the making of a planet or a man; the thought is the cause and the manifestation is the effect. Even the so-called laws of the physical universe are simply the activity of this one law in some form.

What It Does.

Metaphysics, therefore, teaches us how we may govern our bodies, our world, and our happiness by the thoughts we think; for it declares that man reproduces the creative method and that what is true in the macrocosm or universe is true in the microcosm or individual, that thoughts become things. And it claims that by acquiring the knowledge of the law, and by working in harmony with it, man can be freed from limitations of all kinds.

Our subsequent studies will reveal that the creative mind in man, and the creative mind in the universe are not two, but rather essentially one. The value of this understanding is that we may use universal creative forces to secure the good we desire, without feeling that *we* have to create. We do not *make* the law, we *use* it, and it does our work for us.

All healing accordingly, is divine. "It is *done unto us* even as we will," it is not done *by us*. Human will originates its own ideas but Divine Mind creates. The healer is not the source, but the channel; not the light, but the window; not the electricity, but the wire. He is the teacher who will guide to the truth until the patient learns the way for himself.

So all metaphysical healing is based on the principle, that the body of man and his affairs are created by the mind which can either build or destroy, and that this mind is controlled by thought. Jesus was the Supreme Metaphysician because He could speak the word of authority to mind so positively that when He said, "Rise and take up thy bed," the paralytic did as was commanded him to do.

It is evident that Jesus used a law that is open to the use of everybody. The constitution of man has not changed nor his essential nature, and so today men are demonstrating this power. I count it as the greatest work that today engages the attention of mankind—not the mere healing, but the advancement of the knowledge of these things in a world of need.

METAPHYSICS, A SCIENCE.

For it is a knowledge, or as we say, a science or philosophy. And it takes a real mind to understand it. Metaphysics engages the mind. We must *think,* and rich and fruitful are the results of logical thinking. By it we move back along the path of history and science and logical deduction into the realm of Original Causation. We find ourselves entering into the field where all is Spirit in the beginning of things. We see the Spirit or Cosmic Mind taking the initial step in the creation of the universe. We are at a period before Substance or matter is in existence so that we know that the All-Originating Mind could have but one mode of activity—that of thought. By the process of thought Spirit projects a substance as universal as itself which we call ether. By **Acting upon Ether** the Creative Mind brings into being planetary systems, earth and all its myriad forms and life.

To test this we may reverse the process of our thought and begin with science. We take so-called matter and analyze it into its constituent elements, to the molecule, then to the atom, then to the aeon, then to the electron, and finally to primary ether, which science declares to be the ultimate source of matter. Now science cannot tell whence came this ultimate substance, nor how it received its energy. That is the task of metaphysics and metaphysics meets the problem squarely by declaring energy to be the thought of the Creative Mind.

THE UNDERLYING UNITY.

So that whatsoever way we approach our subject we find an underlying unity to all things—ether, from the material standpoint; mind, from the mental. Back of all things then is the Divine Mind or Spirit through whose concept the world springs into existence. *We thus find ourself living in an idealistic universe, a universe which in its essential nature is purely spiritual and therefore subject* to the **Control of Thought Alone.** This is the underlying unity which relates all parts to the great whole—man and nature to the Divine Mind which brought all into existence. It was the great achievement of Moses to discover this underlying unity, or rather to learn it from the Ancient

Egyptian priesthood and reveal it to the Israelitish people. It is the greatest fact or precept of the Old Testament, which led Jesus when asked which was the greatest commandment to quote these words, "Hear, O Israel, the Lord thy God, the Lord is one."

It is the work of metaphysics to show that man can put himself into harmony with this One Originating Source and work in unison with the Creative Purpose, and thus be able to accomplish all things.

REALIZATION.

I am now entered into the consideration of the greatest theme that ever engaged the intellect of man for I am making no less a study than the Way of God with men. I therefore claim from the Divine Intelligence that makes and sustains the universe, the necessary mental capacity and intuition to perceive the great truths of metaphysics. I hold that only the truth will appeal to me and that no error of false judgment will be able to enter my mind to stay there. No previous thought or prejudice shall be allowed to influence me against reason in my study of the new order. I dare to go all the way with truth for Truth is God and God is all. So far as I see the light, I will follow it, and I shall not think that the traditions of men are of more value than my own logical conclusions. I commit my ways and my thoughts to God, I trust in the divine illumination which can come to my own soul and I venture out in faith on the new pathways of understanding. I will fear no

evil, for Thou art with me. I now claim the nea
and dear presence of Divine Love and Wisdom.
rejoice in the Heart of the World and in my shar
in the activities of the Divine Creative Mind. Thou
O Lord, art with me alway even unto the ends of th
earth. I worship and bow down, I kneel before th
Lord my God. I am at one with Infinite Life, Love
and Wisdom and I give thanks for the light that no
begins to illumine my pathway.

LESSON II. 21

THE ONE LAW WE NEED TO KNOW.

THERE is one law supreme to this system of
life. Sometimes we call it "the law of cause
and effect." Sometimes we speak of it as the method
by which spirit passes into manifestation. Psycholo-
gists frequently speak of it as the law of suggestion.
Every teacher of metaphysics spends his time either
in giving his interpretation of it or in explaining some
truth that is related to it. Our happiness and success
in life are measured by the degree to which either
consciously or unconsciously we are obedient to the
requirements of this law. It is the law that we cannot break, but we can be broken by trying to break it.
It is the law by which "as ye sow, ye also shall reap."
Through it, "it shall be done unto you according to
your faith." It explains why "as a man thinketh in
his heart, so is he." It is the basis of the "law of
correspondences." It is the activity of Creative Mind,
neither good nor bad, by which we create our own
heaven and our own hell. It is the secret of all trag-
edy and all comedy. It is the touchstone to truth,
and he who knows it and employs it wisely is the
emancipated soul and a master on the path. Let the
student therefore learn the following principles which
constitute the law that through the knowledge he may

15

obtain the mastery of fate and control the conditions
of life and destiny; for no less a power is in the
hands of him who learns and wisely employs this law.
All must use it because we live by it; but how few
use it wisely.

THE LAW.

1. The first principle of this law is that of *the universal presence of intelligence;* that we live, move and
have our being in a vast sea of life, both visible and
invisible; that this intelligent life is not only around
us but is in us; even more, it not only is around and
in us, but it is the substance as well of which all things
(including our bodies) are composed. This statement
is supported alike by revelation, as in the Bible; by
science, as in psychology or chemistry; and by philosophy, as in our lesson on Spirit.

Before there was a visible universe which we call
"Nature" there must of necessity have been an invisible universe which we call Spirit or Power. The
orderly way in which It arranged the visible universe
which It created shows that It was and is a Wonderful
Intelligence.

Since Spirit was (and is) all, it had nothing else
than itself out of which to make a world. It therefore
had to fashion a substance for its own body—the universe—out of itself, or Spirit. Since Spirit is Intelligence, of necessity the substance which it brought
forth must share its nature. And all life must mani
fest the life of Spirit since it proceeds from it. All
science is agreed that life has never been discovered

that did not come from antecedent life, so that we can move back from the life of Nature to the life from which it is derived, or Nature's God. Accordingly Nature and the life in Nature are one and the same thing and we live in a universe which is literally *alive*.

2. We see, therefore, that *this Universal Intelligence is also creative.* It is the power that makes things, and is the intelligence that moulds original substance and holds it in form. As in man the subjective or impersonal mind builds new life cells day by day and takes care of the growing life of the child and the renewing life of maturity, so in Nature, the Creative Mind is busy building ever more stately mansions for its dwelling place. New universes are being flung out across the vast abyss of space; new stars begin to gleam as they launch out on their ageless journey around some distant sun; the earth upon which we tread is growing daily through the addition of cosmic dust and daily changing in its internal structure; new forms of life are appearing or old are altering; flowers are blooming into life to breathe their beauty on the breast of nature; and we live in a world of life, ever-renewing, ever-changing, ever-evolving into higher expression of the exhaustless energy of Creative Mind. *The second part of our law therefore calls attention to the fact that we not only live in a world of intelligence, but that this intelligence is constantly creating.* "Behold I make all things new." In this is man's hope and his power to act.

This life is the life of the Creative Spirit, Intelligence, or Mind, and therefore we perceive that It emerges into form to enjoy its own Power-to-Live. When we think, it is Spirit thinking through us; when we utter a truth it is Spirit putting out into expression a thought from its limitless Power-to-Think; when we breathe it is Spirit breathing *us*.

3. *This creative intelligence acts upon the impress of the strongest impression, thought, or image, made upon it.*

When man emerges in consciousness out of this vast sea of life, as a wave runs upon the bosom of the ocean, he rises sufficiently high to enable him to perceive that there is an ocean. Thus Spirit fulfills a purpose in becoming man by enabling Itself, through becoming the particular, to perceive Itself in its All-ness. Man is spirit come forth out of the formless into form, out of the timeless into time, out of the limitless into certain limitations, and yet, as man, spirit never loses its power to draw upon its resources as Spirit. Therefore, we must recognize that *all the power of the universe is back of the mind of man when he thinks.*

Then, too, we must recognize that there cannot be a will in the Universal Mind opposed to man, for if there were, then he could not draw from the creative mind and power what he wants except by chance. We therefore recognize that so far as we are concerned there is back of us a Universal Creative Mind which desires to become to us whatever we desire, that is whatever we think into it, and which has no purposes of its own opposed to ours. As It creates a world by thinking a world, (for Mind can act only through thought) so it creates for man himself, whatever he desires, by acting as Creative Mind upon his thought. This Mind, therefore, *is in this aspect purely impersonal and neutral* (see Lesson VII). It has no purposes of its own as opposed to ours. It is *creative activity,* infinitely susceptible, responsive to our every thought (Lesson V) *and is the power that brings into existence in form whatever we fashion in thought.*

We therefore perceive that whatever we think must make a greater or lesser impression on Creative Mind and that when we consciously use our knowledge *we make an image of the thing we desire; then we present it to the Great Creative Intelligence which begins to act upon our suggestion to bring forth our good into visible form.* The purpose of this book in the main is to show the various phases of the activity of this law, the law of **Creative Activity**, by which the creative mind brings into form whatever we present to it sufficiently forcefully in thought.

4. But there is one other feature of the Law which must not be overlooked. This is what we may term the personal side of Spirit's activity. While, as law, it acts in the manner we have just described; and while, so far as the individual will is concerned, it does not act contrary to our purposes, still it also acts as a law of tendency. It tends to the production of higher manifestations of itself in individual expression and form. It is seeking its own self-expression since

there can be no other motive of creation at all. Its nature is life, love, and wisdom. This it seeks to man_ ifest. Accordingly it stands back of man as the source of his life, love, and wisdom, and is ready to "teach us all things and guide us in the way of truth." It not only creates, therefore, according to the thought we impress upon it as law or Impersonal Mind, but *It becomes the director of man's thought and life,* whenever we turn to it for guidance and direction in our affairs. (See Lessons XXVIII to XXXI.)

This is in accordance with the three principles just outlined, for, *as Infinite Wisdom, it takes the impress of our desire for Wisdom and brings that out into expression* just as it does life and form./We perceive this Intelligence therefore as the source of man's inspirations and intuitions. When we turn for guidance to It, It becomes our teacher and guide. When we turn to It for love, It becomes our Lover. The greatest achievement of our own highest intelligence is therefore to be found in so harmonizing ourselves with this great Life, Love, and Wisdom that we may find It in us as a perennial spring, the water of life surging up eternally from the depth of our being. "Whosoever believes on this spirit of life, from within him shall flow springs of living water."

(Make a study of all the facts you know in relation to this great law. Restate it in your own words. Learn it in some such form as this:

1. I live in a universe of Intelligence in which everything is alive and infinitely responsive to thought,

since it takes its form out of the substance of Mind through the process of thinking.

2. This Intelligence is the *Creative* Factor in all Nature and in the moulding of all thought into form.

3. It creates according to its own thought and according to the strongest impression or image of thought of the individual mind.

4. It is the source of my life and understanding and impresses its nature and wisdom upon me as I allow it, through my intuitions.

Therefore, I control my life and conditions by the thoughts I think, since the Universal Mind acts creatively on my every thought. I am, through my power of thought, master of my fate.)

REALIZATION.

Meditate on the above law. Think how your life has been controlled either by your own thinking or by the suggestions that have been made upon your mind, either consciously or unconsciously. When you were a child you took your thought from your family. Your world was what you made it, but it was an unconscious acceptance of the thought and manners of your family. After a while you began to think independently and your world changed that much for you. You began to control *consciously* the conditions of your life. As your understanding grew you thought more and more independently of your associates, therefore your life became that much different from theirs. Did you continue to accept the sug-

gestions of your environment or did you begin to
think independently? Either consciously or unconsciously you are now conditioning your life.

I will now take conscious control of my life. I will
think only the things I want to think. I will control
whatever is to come into my life, by controling my
thought. I will daily mould my thoughts into finer
form that Creative Mind in me and around me may
bring forth a world for me of fairer form. I will
think thoughts of truth, that I may be guided by
Supreme Wisdom; I will think thoughts of faith that
I may have the peace of God that passeth all understanding. I do now so think. I am filled with the
spirit of love. I am in harmony with the Divine
Mind. I am open and receptive to the highest feelings.
I do now consciously contact the Mind of Love and
Wisdom. I wait on the Lord that He may renew my
strength. My mind is stayed on Thee and I am at
perfect peace with all men, and with myself. No
evil can befall me and the angels of love are round
about me. Conscious of the godlike qualities of my
soul, I go my way today in the strength of the Infinite.
I walk upon the earth as master and not as slave. I
keep the law and the law keeps me. I obey the law
and the law obeys me. I give my heart to God in
divinest joy of self-giving and I feel the helping hand
of God upon me. I am glad, I am strong, I am full
of life and love today.

LESSON III.

HOW TO USE THE LAW—THE SILENCE.

THE best results are to be secured by using the Law so far as we know it while at the same time looking for more light. The student who approaches this subject for the first time has as yet little to work on for he has not tested out the Law by science and experience. But enough has been said to make us realize that the object of a treatment is to impress our desire on the creative Law with sufficient force to register in the Creative Mind. If the Law creates for us according to the thoughts we think into Mind, then what we must do is to raise our consciousness to the highest pitch of expectancy so that the best possible results may be secured. Accordingly we must realize that the first thing for us to do in a treatment is to impress *our own mind* with the feeling that we are about to act upon the Law and that it is about to act for us.

1. The right atmosphere for a treatment, therefore, is that of high faith, so that we will do well to bring ourselves up to the proper pitch of expectancy by some preliminary reading. Take the Bible and read the precious promises in it. "Lo I am with you alway, even unto the end of the world." "Who for giveth all thine iniquities, who healeth all thy dis-

eases." "They that trust in the Lord shall renew
their strength, they shall mount up with wings as
eagles; they shall run and not be weary; they shall
walk and not faint " "According to your faith be it
done unto you." "Ask, and ye shall receive; seek, and
ye shall find; knock, and it shall be opened unto you."
"When ye pray, believe that ye have received, and
ye shall receive." Go over such passages as will help
you to strong faith. Learn some of the best ones.
One should memorize something daily—a verse, a
stanza of poetry, a statement of truth. Everybody
should know the Twenty-Third and the Ninety-First
Psalm and be able to repeat it at such times as needed
to strengthen confidence.

It will also be of great help to read for a few minutes or longer in some helpful book of truth. The
student may well read "Creative Mind" or "Being and
Becoming." The purpose of this book is, of course,
to furnish both instruction and inspiration. After
reading the lesson for the day, you will *feel* the truth
more keenly.

2. Having prepared yourself in faith and knowledge, the course of your thought might well run along
the line of the Law, much like this: "I know that I
am surrounded by the finer forces of Spirit. (Lessons
IV and VI.) I know that I myself am a center of
conscious activity in this great ocean of Divine Mind.
(Lessons V and VI.) I know that my word has become the word of truth and a model of creation for
the Creative Mind for the good I desire. (Lessons

XII and XVI.) Go on mentally meditating along these lines so long as you feel the interest or need.

If necessary overcome any feeling that may arise of fear or uncertainty.

3. Rid yourself of any sense of sin or fault. If you feel that you have done wrong in any way, seek to right it so that you may have a clear consciousness. "If therefore thou art offering thy gift at the altar, and there rememberest that thy brother has aught against thee (cause for it, in your wronging him), leave thy gift before the altar, and go thy way; first be reconciled to thy brother, and then come and offer thy gift." These are the words of the Master Metaphysician, and reveal the necessity of no counter thought against that of pure faith. If necessary, forgive yourself for anything you have done that you feel to have been wrong. The son of man has power on earth to forgive sin. You are a son of man.

If you have fear, get rid of it in the same way. Cast it out. There is nothing to fear. Pull out all the weeds of wrong thinking. Declare that evil or the thought of evil has no influence over you.

4. Now *feel* as deeply as you can that all is well with you and the world. Feel how good it is to know this freeing truth; to know that you are a child of God; to know that "all power is given unto me in heaven and on earth." To know that "greater work than these shall ye do because I go unto my Father."

Then say, "I am pure spirit living in a world of spirit and guarded by the Great Spirit of Life." God is spirit and they that worship Him must worship Him in spirit and in truth. I am now entered in spirit and in truth into the higher, finer places where I am in contact with all that is. I would see and know the truth and feel it at this hour. As a child of the Living God, I make my claim upon the Law. Let this good (mentioning it) come to me.

5. Say distinctly and with deep feeling just what you want of the Law. You are not dictating to it, but if you do not know what you want, the Law has nothing to work on. At the same time, what you are after is the *idea* of the thing, so you may be sure that the Greater Wisdom will give you only the thing that will be for your best good, but it will be the thing you want and will be along the line for which you were holding the faith attitude

6. Expect greatly and you will receive greatly. Be strong in your faith, so strong that you feel in your heart that it is now done unto you even as you think, and you can give thanks for it. "Make known your request unto God with thanksgiving." "In everything give thanks." Be grateful.

7. For those who wish to develop spiritual perception which is the basis of the highest healing power, it is desirable to dwell on the thought of Spirit as a Living Presence breathing in and through us, vitally interested in all our affairs and identifying itself with all our highest purposes, and aspirations. The desires we have are then recognized as those of Spirit seeking its own self-expression. The love we have

is the love of Spirit in us, and the life is but the individual manifestation of that larger life in which we share.

The true "Silence" is the quiet realization of Spirit with such intensity of feeling that we are merged in the Great All and are one with the Infinite Mind. In this consciousness we may secure the highest results by simply being still and knowing that the Father gives us all things even before we ask Him. "Before they call I will answer them." "The Spirit knoweth what things ye have need of before ye ask them."

The Final Purpose of These Lessons Is Nothing Less than to Bring up the Consciousness of the Seeker for Truth to the Point Where the Demonstration Is Made by Simply Knowing in His Heart that the Good He Seeks Is His Now Simply Because He Has Thought It. That Is the Way in Which Creative Mind Makes Things, and in the End that Is the Way We Must Secure Them. We Must Know That Our Thoughts Manifest as Things. This Will Free Us from All Sense of Struggle. This Is the Final Peace of the Soul and the Great Goal of Individual Life—to Have the Enjoyment of Self-Conscious Existence and Yet to Rest in the Infinite and Eternal Calm of the Divine Mind.

Says Edward Roland Sill:

  " 'Tis not in seeking,
   'Tis not in endless striving
  Thy quest is found
   Be still and listen:

Be still and drink the quiet
  Of all around.
Not for thy crying,
  Not for thy loud beseeching,
Will peace draw near;
  Rest with palms folded
Rest with thine eyelids fallen—
  Lo! peace is here."

REALIZATION.

I rise to the work and the life of the new day with strength and courage. I go forth with eagerness to my task. I go gladly, blithely on, for at the heart of me God presses in to keep me full supplied with all I need. I will not today lose conscious contact with the life of the Spirit in me. I shall know all day that "beneath me are the girders of the Almighty, under neath are the everlasting arms." Whatever comes to me cannot find me unprepared. If I need wisdom, I have it. If I need courage, I possess it. If I need strength, it is within. My inner life is one with God. "From within me flow streams of living water." "The spirit of truth shall teach me all things and guide me in the way of truth." I am held in infinite security. I have the wonderful poise and strength of one who is conscious of his inner source of strength. Men who see me today shall wonder at my out-breathing force and magnetic power, but I shall know that it is because the strength of the Infinite is in me. So be it.

LESSON IV.

SPIRIT.

SPIRIT is the power that makes things. Like the power of electricity or the affinity that holds the atoms together, or the life in the flower, it cannot be seen, for the simple reason that *Spirit is one and the same as these.* When we see things we perceive them as the form into which Spirit has moulded itself. Back of them lies the power that made them and supports their existence. Spirit then is not a *thing* or a person but a *power.* Yet its power is the power of Mind, for It must exist *before* It manifests in a material universe. Its power accordingly is that of thought and we may therefore say that Spirit is the Power that Knows, the Mind that Thinks, or the Intelligence that Creates. What we call the Life Principle in the plant or animal which causes it to exist and grow is therefore a divine and universal intelligence. It is Spirit or Mind at work.

> All the world is alive
> And throbs with a pulse divine;
> A sentient Mind sustains,
> The soul of it all is God.
> All Nature seems to strive—
> The sap that stirs in the vine,
> The germ that lives in the grain,
> The bud that sprouts on the rod.

29

Unity of Spirit.

We live in a living universe vibrant with the intelligent activity of the Creative Spirit. For the intelligence in the rock, the plant, or man have the same source and at the foundation are one. Otherwise we should be living in a universe of many powers and intelligences which would not be able to understand each other and would, therefore, be in constant discord. But science reveals the fact of a universal harmony and adjustment of parts in perfect order. That man can understand this order proves that there is a Mind—and only one—in it which is like his own.

Nature of Spirit.

This universal Mind or Intelligence is also to be described as Love for all its laws are beneficent and kindly-disposed toward man. The fire beneficently warms us and cooks our food; the sun gladly gives us its light, and life; electricity is our friend and toils for us to produce light and heat and power. It is only when we reverse the natural order, which is that of the Divine Mind or Spirit, that the fire destroys our dwelling, the sun smites with its heat, and the electricity rends us. So the power of the universe which is Spirit is also kind· "He sends his rain on the evil and the good, and his sun to shine on the just and the unjust." He is the Tender Shepherd, the Wonderful Counselor, the Everlasting Father.

SPIRIT AS WISDOM.

As Divine Intelligence Spirit is also the wisdom which directs our affairs, and leads us in green pastures and beside still waters, when we seek Its guidance.

Spirit is therefore the Life that lives us, the love that keeps us and the wisdom that guides us. The Great Heart of the Universe vibrates throughout the cosmic plan and we are held by a "love that will not let us go."

REALIZATION.

Today I look at my world as my friend: The stars are the eyes of God that watch me, the winds and the brooks are the voice of God that speaks to me, the forces of Nature are the Intelligence that serves me. I shall not fear today because I walk in a world I understand, in the presence of Spirit which understands me. I draw upon the hidden energies and power of Spirit. I am in harmony with it all. (Now repeat the 23rd Psalm.) Surely I am led by all love and wisdom in the paths of peace. ✓ "When thou passeth through the waters, I will be with thee; and through the rivers, they shall not overflow thee; when thou walkest through the fire, thou shalt not be burned, neither shall the flame kindle upon thee." No forces are opposed to me because I recognize in them all the activity of Spirit, loving me, guiding me, giving me new life, today.

"God's in his heaven—and his creation—and all's right with my world."

LESSON V.

CREATIVE MIND IN THE INDIVIDUAL.

WE have already seen that there is a universally present creative intelligence; and the fact that we can recognize it shows that the intelligence in us which cognizes it must be of the same kind. What the nature of the intelligence is which we observe, and the relation of the mind of the individual to the cosmic mind, we will investigate in this and the following chapter. The modern study of experimental psychology has revealed much that is of assistance to the student of metaphysics regarding the nature of the individual mind, and by analogy, at least, of the universal mind. We find that man is possessed of a mind with two distinct ways of acting. The two phases of activity are called subjective and objective.* Close study reveals the essential unity of these activities and their interaction, in such a way as to prove that it is a unitary mind that acts in either case. The objective mind is that which man develops to enable him to contact his environment and maintain himself in a world of form and sensation. The babe is born into the world purely subjective. It probably does not use its objective

---

*Note. We use the terms *subjective* and *objective* mind for the sake of comparison, and the word *subconscious* as a synonym for *subjective*. While this is not entirely scientific it better answers the purpose of the work we are doing here.

faculties until it contacts an objective environment. But at the moment of its birth, its objective faculties begin to develop. It feels the cold for the sensory nerve system which is the agent of objective mind carries that impression to its brain. This sensory system is designed to enable the mind to contact its environment and protect the body through the sensations and warnings that are registered by it. As time goes on the child develops a full set of objective activities largely by imitation of the movements, voice, and manners of its elders. In early years, environment makes a child; in later years he makes it. The objective mind with the sensory nerve system under its control governs most of the activities of the voluntary muscles. If I raise my hand to strike the keys of the piano, I do it by an act of will of the objective mind. In time, however, through repeated acts, a habit of action is formed, and then the movement is done unconsciously or under the direction of the subconscious mind.

The subjective or subconscious mind, therefore, is found to control the involuntary functions of the body such as the beating of the heart, the contraction and expansion of the lungs, and the digestion of food. We do not have to think consciously about these things; they are done unconsciously. The important fact about the subconscious mind is this: *it is the builder of the body,* or *the creative mind.* Under its direction new life cells are constantly being born to take the place of those which have finished their work and are passing away. New heart cells are born each minute, new lung cells, new nerve tissues. As every action consumes energy and thus produces waste in the system, the subconscious mind must busy itself with carrying away the waste through the blood, pores, kidneys, lungs, and waste system, and at the same time go about to build new life cells to take the place of the old. Our fingers, for example, would soon wear out if they were made of steel, but being made of living flesh, they need never wear out for they are repaired daily by the builder of the body. Thus a marvelous activity is constantly going on within us, asleep or awake, of which we are entirely unconscious; and a million servants of the system are each scurrying to his appointed place to do his workman-like task. So it is literally true that "every day is a fresh beginning, every morn is the world made new," for we rise with a renewed body which is so frequently reconstructed that every organ and tissue is doubtless born anew in the course of one year or less. While the healer is never conscious of this activity and would no more think of trying to direct it than the president of a railroad would try to boss a section gang, at the same time it is because this activity takes place that a new body can be "demonstrated"; for under the stimulus of faith and understanding a definite impression of health is made on each new cell as it is born and thus the organ is made whole. All these recreative agents are very susceptible to mental attitudes and reflect our thought either for health or disease. For example, the blood is known to contain certain agents for the destruction of dangerous germs (a germ being an objectified disease thought). These agents customarily approach the foreigner, encircle him, literally cover him with sauce to make him palatable and proceed to eat him. But if the individual is mentally depressed and negative, the little guardian of the body reflects his attitude, does not cover the germ with sauce and refuses to eat him. Then trouble ensues. This scientific fact shows the Bible to be correct when it says, "As a man thinketh in his heart, so is he" in his body.

> My world was empty, cold, and chill,
>   And all-unkind,
> The while there waited on my will,
>   Creative Mind
> With unused powers of vastest good;
>   Yet all-unsought.
> THE VISION CAME, I understood,
>   I THOUGHT A THOUGHT:
> And, by that thought, my world, ablaze,
>   Flared into form:
> And, by that thought, from primal haze, ✔
>   Love, tender, warm,
> Was flashed in splendor to my soul
>   No more in fear,
> While angels wrote on heaven's scroll,
>   "A Christ is here."

This Mind Impersonal and Controlled by Impressions.

That the creative activities reflect our mental attitudes, as we see so plainly from these examples, proves another interesting fact, that *the subconscious mind and its functioning is entirly under the control of impressions made upon it.* That is, it acts as the creative agent, *naturally* along the line of health and re-creation, which is *native to it;* but, on the other hand, it has no purpose of its own apart from the objective mind; and if the objective mind gives it impressions of disease, imperfection, fear, worry, pain, and so on, it begins at once to create accordingly. We see, therefore, that the subconscious or creative mind is entirely *impersonal;* it has no purposes of its own. Again, it is subject to control by suggestion; and, finally, it is entirely deductive.

Deductive.

By deductive, we mean that it takes any suggestion given it and then works out the complete idea without any further help from the objective mind. Many persons have had the experience of learning a rule or principle in mathematics but could not solve a problem by it. On going to sleep, however, they have given the problem over to subconscious mind, only to awaken during the night with the problem all solved. The sleepless mind, with perfect deductive power, has worked it all out for them.

The value of this fact to the healer is that he knows that when he gives a treatment he does not need to lie awake nights holding the thought. All he has to do is to give the idea or concept of perfect health to the mind, which will begin at once to carry it out in perfect expression in the body. (See Lesson XVI).

The student should retain these facts about his mind: *it is creative, impersonal* and *deductive.* In Lesson XXIX he will also find how it *acts intuitively* by contacting universal mind and appropriating its resources. In Lesson XIV he can study it as the *seat of the emotions.* It is the mind that never forgets; it also is *clairvoyant* and *clairaudient;* and *can convey and receive* telepathic messages,——a fact now recognized scientifically.

Finally, it is through this mind that man makes his approach to the universal; for, as we shall see in the succeeding chapter, this mind and the universal share in a common nature, since both are creative, impersonal and deductive. This mind does its work not as a separate part but as an individual activity of the universal. It is through it that the universal is able to act on the plane of the particular. It is through the expansion of man's consciousness of the inner qualities of this mind that he is able at length to contact the universal and through it he may hope ultimately to know the truth. Man cannot bring God down to his level but through the inner mind he may hope to rise to the point where he may more universally comprehend the Infinite. If the student will bear this in mind, that his work is the extension of his own consciousness to grasp the Infinite, he will be urged to the highest endeavor as well as filled with the loftiest inspirations.

> "Were I so tall to reach the pole
>   Or grasp the ocean with my span,
>   I would be measured by my soul;
>   The mind's the standard of the man."

Nor should we fail to remind ourselves that there is no real separation between what we call the objective mind and the subjective of the individual. We shall then perceive that the objective is the outer expression of the real self which we have been studying under the term "subconscious." Then when we perceive that the real self is the Mind of the Infinite finding concrete expression in us as the wave finds concrete expression on the bosom of the ocean, we are prepared to feel the essential unity of all being and to enter into the realization of the Master, "I say ye are gods."

In this perception, man may rise to heights never before attained for it is the emancipation proclamation of his soul. No more is he who realizes it bound by creeds, confessions, precedents or traditions. He is free with a glad freedom. His life is complete, for he is at one with the All-Life. His wisdom is supreme, for the Spirit is his teacher. Freed of all fetters, his soul may soar to heights imperial and sublime until he stands with the sons of God at the gates of the City Celestial.

REALIZATION.

I rise to the consciousness of the godlike nature of my own soul. I am today conscious of my union with the God and Father of us all, who is over all, through all, and in us all. In this high consciousness I dare to make claim on the best of all there is. I make no ignorant claims of power for "I know Him in whom I have believed." I know and dare to assert the magnificent powers of my manhood. And if I have not yet brought out all my latent powers, still I will claim their possession and press on toward the mark of the high calling of God in my own soul. I am one with Life, I am one with Wisdom, I am one with Love. All that the Father hath is mine; and I glory in the independence of my soul from every thing, while I rest in the consciousness that there is no separation between me and the Father. If I have felt any such separation, I now cast it out from me forever and go on in the joy of my eternal union with All-Good, my Lord and my God. I am thankful for this perception of my own soul.

LESSON VI.

CREATIVE MIND IN THE UNIVERSAL.

LESSONS II and IV have already paved the way for the statement that we can discover in the universe the presence of a mind exactly corresponding to that of the individual which we have just studied. The presence of a universal order in nature reveals an intelligence like our own, for nothing less than the presence of a creative and sustaining intelligence can account for such a miracle of accuracy of interrelated parts. This intelligence is at the root of all things and its method of activity is what we call the law of nature. In the cosmos it works with such absolute precision that man's very life depends upon it, as in the law of the attraction of gravitation and gravity, centrifugal and centripetal motion, or in the law of electricity, or the principle of growth. That man can dominate his universe and his environment proves that at its heart is an intelligence like his own or he could not control it. Again it is known that the mind or thought of the individual can act to move ponderable objects as, for example, we find in Lesson VIII. It is interesting to note that other objects than metals have been known to be moved by thought. Not to mention the miracles of Jesus, we may call attention to the records of the Society for Psychical Research.

That a metal can be controlled by thought and magnetized by it, shows that a corresponding intelligence inheres in it. The study of botany is very fruitful of illustration of this cosmic or atomic intelligence. Biology and the investigation of cell life, to which we have already referred, point to definite conclusions. One may read an interesting story in the life of the *moneron,* the lowest form of independent life, perceiving its purposeful activity in approaching a one-cell plant and deciding whether or not it can swallow it. If it finds the cell too large, it moves away to another. It inflates its body with gas to rise in the water or deflates it to sink again. Many other marvels are recorded of it by science. The organized social life of the bee is illustrative. Maeterlinck's story is a romance of Divine Mind with the "Spirit of the hive" showing purposeful activity, not for the sake of the individual life of the bee but for the sake of the corporate life and for the preservation of the swarm.

One need not mention the instinct of the beaver with its mechanical engineering ability, nor the dog or the horse with their superior instinct. Law in mechanics and instinct in animals alike betray the universal Cosmic Mind at work.

The Universal Mind—Subconscious.

We have already seen that the material universe is the outward manifestation of the inner power of spirit. Spirit, we said, is the Power-to-Create, it is the power

that makes things, but it works as the law of growth
from within. This shows that the universal mind is
subjective (or subconscious). That it is subjective is
shown by the fact that it is a unit, as we have seen in
Lesson IV; and since it is a unit, it acts independently
of *form* or *individuality;* and as it acts independently of
individual *volition,* it cannot have an objective mind or
personal activity in the ordinary sense. (See Lesson
XXVIII.) Again we perceive that the cosmic mind
is subjective since it is creative. Finally we discern
that its activities are *deductive* for this reason: In-
ductive reasoning is based on the study of the various
facts and phenomena of life from which a law or principle is induced, as for example, Newton finds that a
falling apple, a sun, and a moon all act in a similar
fixed way and from it induces the law of attraction of
gravitation. Now the universal creative mind cannot
act by induction since at the beginning of the creative
series it has no facts or phenomena on which to base
its inductions. Forms have not yet been brought into
manifestation. At the same time it can act by deduction since deduction is the method by which we move
in argument from a fixed principle or law to varied
conclusions. Spirit itself is fixed Principle or Law,
and so it creates form and manifestation by logical de-
ductions from its own Principle. It fashions a rose in
thought, for when the creative series begins it has no
rose to use for a pattern. It thinks a star into form
and it begins to shine, or a bird and it begins to sing.
As *form* takes rise out of the thought of creative mind,

we perceive that this mind is deductive and impersonal as well as creative.

It is necessary in a book of short lessons like this to cover these points without a great deal of argument, but sufficient is said here to point the student in the right direction. By study of the other chapters he may make the foregoing principles clearer, but the object of this lesson is to show him that *both his own sub-conscious mind and that of the universe are creative, impersonal, and deductive,* i. e., each acts with perfect creative intelligence to produce in form and manifesta tion whatever impression is made upon it. The ob jective mind is found to have its rise or origin in the subjective, is developed in the individual to enable him to contact and control his environment; and then the subjective turns about to act as its servant to carry out its orders, and objectify its desires. When the student has acquired knowledge of these facts, he has become master of the first principles of metaphysics and can hopefully press on with these weapons in his hand to the mastery of his universe. For these are the results of them that believe and know:

1. The body is controlled for health and happiness by giving the creative mind within only the highest and most perfect ideas and ideals. *If you do not know what is best to suggest to it, shut out all negative thoughts and let it alone;* its tendency is toward health, and "the spirit knoweth what things ye have need of before ye ask them." (Lesson XXIX.)

2. Since we live in a unitary universe (See Lesson

X *et al.,*) our own inner mind is at one with the Infinite
and we may therefore control our conditions of prosperity and environment as well as our health. Our objective mind gives the impression or image to the
universal subconscious; and the latter acts to produce
for us just what we think. In practical demonstration
all we have to do is to forget the terms, "subconscious,"
"objective," etc., and just go to work to realize the
truth for ourselves. This book is simply designed to
tell us something of *how* it occurs, but we must beware
of thinking of ourselves as having to "create," "work,"
"struggle," or "do" something. We simply identify
ourselves with the good we desire and then expect it.
(See my book on "Being and Becoming.")

3. We can work independently of all antecedent
conditions: there are no limitations in creative mind,
no modifiers, no competition, no lack of any kind. All
Is; and That Is All. Then, too, the element of time
does not come in, since in the realm of spirit there
is no time. Space does not matter for we are dealing
with a medium where space is unknown. Material or
physical distance is no barrier because there is none
in spirit; and it is as easy to get results in healing with
the patient a thousand miles away as a few feet. We
do not send out thoughts for there is nowhere to send
them. Everywhere is right here. We do not need to
pump up power from some exterior source for omni-
potence is here in its entirety when we recognize it;
since as a unit with the Father, I may say, "All power
is given unto me in heaven and on earth."

4. Destruction, disease, death, and all the ills of life come from a sense of separation from the All-Life. There can be no real separation since all is one; but a feeling of separateness is at the base of all discord and unhappiness. To restore health, wealth, and love, therefore, it is necessary only to make our unity with life, with Universal Mind, with the "God and Father of us all who is over all, through all and in you all"; for Universal Mind is to those who are conscious of their union with It no less than the God and Father of us all. In this we should find the most splendid inspiration; for mental science does not rob God of any of those essential qualities which our hearts crave of Him but rather enlarges our concept of His power and our own, at the same time. As Sam Walter Foss says:

"As wider skies broke on his view
God greatened in his growing mind,
Each year he dreamed his God anew
And left his older God behind.

He saw the boundless scheme dilate
In star and blossom, sky and clod,
And as the universe grew great,
He dreamed for it a greater God."

REALIZATION.

Take the above four statements and meditate upon them.

I now make my conscious union with the All-Good. I will no longer feel a sense of separateness. I will rejoice in my divine rights as a son in the Father's house. (I will arise and go unto my Father. Today I am conscious of the Indwelling Presence of Divine Life, Love, and Wisdom. I realize that my world is but a reflection of my own thought, and I think only the best, the purest and the truest. I look for my good in all things and I find good in all people. I am filled with wisdom and the power of Spirit. I am at one with the Life of the World and I am glad. (Then "ask what ye will and it shall be done unto you." Give thanks.)

LESSON VII.

MAN, MASTER ON THE PLANET.

TO describe man as he truly and divinely is, is to describe God in a great variety of his attributes. Jesus, the most divinely human and the most humanly divine Being who ever came into this world, typifies the attributes which man shares with God. God is Love, Truth, Life, Activity, Intelligence, Spirit. In all this man shares with God. He is made in the divine image: God breathed into him the breath of life and he became a living soul. And it is only as man recognizes his own true nature and manifests his own inner powers that he can rise to the sublime heights which Jesus reached and dominate all physical conditions.

Most of all he must recognize his own spiritual nature. This is the great imperative. (Man himself is spirit.) The real man, the *ego*, is not the human body, nor the human mind; it is the *life* or divine mind within, the eternal essence of being which springs from God. This inner or divine life, which is the real man, partakes of the nature of God. It shares his intelligence, comprehends his truths, is co-eternal with his life, and co-operates in his activity—"my Father worketh hitherto; and I work." This inner life is complete and whole, unlimited in all the essentials of true being.

Such is man, and it is only as he realizes and acts

47

upon these truths that he enters into the rich heritage and privileges of health and peace and plenty. And it is to restore him to a consciousness of his divine being or sonship that the Spirit is ever acting. Such was the mission of Jesus, such is the activity of the Holy Spirit or Comforter, "who shall teach you all things and guide you in the way of truth." The one great, distinctive message of Jesus was that God is Father and man is son. To the Mosaic message of the One Unity he adds the Infinite Multiplicity whose organic relationship he demonstrated. "I and the Father are one." "That they may all be one, even as we are one; I in them, and thou in me, that they may be perfected into one."

THE SECRET OF MAN'S MASTERY.

This is in truth the great secret, but no *mystery,* of man's mastery over all conditions. When he comes to realize his spiritual nature, his kinship and unity with God, and acts with reason and convinced faith upon this knowledge, he has mastered the problem of life and destiny. So Jesus mastered it; and so are many men and women today learning how to control destiny.

It is all here: God, Eternal Spirit acting through the power of thought upon a spiritual universe to create and recreate: man, in nature, mind and being, like God, acting in like manner upon a spiritual creation, plastic to *his* mind, securing similar results in body, mind and estate.

Let us then realize that we are sons and daughters

of God and so realizing secure all the benefits of this relationship. Remember that apart from Him we can do nothing but that " *with* God all things are possible." This then is the supreme thought for us to realize.

"I live in His Eternal Life
And know His life is mine."

His life is mine—and all that that life contains is mine also!

We thus see that we live in a spiritual universe and that man himself is in essence and nature a spiritual being, fashioned in the image and likeness of God and sharing his attributes. As such a being, he himself can dominate what we call physical forces and energies, for God gave him dominion. In no essential is this more true than in relation to the physical organism which we call our body. It is immediately in the control of the inner principle of life which we call our self.

We have too long spoken of ourselves as "weak human flesh," "creatures of the dust," "doomed to decay," and kindred destructive names. As we eventually become what we think, we have indeed manifested all the weakness to which we are willing to make our flesh heir. But it ought not to be so, and the way to change our condition is to immediately change our thought.

Shall you say, "My body rules me. This *leg* tells me *I* cannot walk. This *hand* tells me *I* cannot write. This *ear* tells me *I* cannot hear. I must do what my leg and hand and ear tell me"? Shall you yield organ by organ to what you think that organ tells you until you become like the man of whom Bishop Sabin wrote that he claimed to have "lost the use of both lungs and had to breathe through his stomach"? Or will you not rather say, "I manifest physically what I am mentally; I, therefore, the true self, do now say to you, Leg, walk; Arm, write; Ear, listen"?

Your pain is not in your leg but in your mind; your deafness is not in your ear but in your thought. And when the thought has been completely changed, you will find that there is no pain at all. It is indeed all a matter of consciousness. If God made a perfect creation, He did not make a pain in it. It is inconceivable that in wanton caprice He should have said, "Here is a foot: I will put a pain in that. Here is an arm: I will paralyze that. Here is a good man, but I will just double up his body with rheumatism." Did God do that? Certainly not! And if He did not, who did? Wrong thinking did.

REVERSING OUR THOUGHT.

But does not this reverse the accepted philosophy of the race and its interpretation of human experiences? I hope so. For who would wish to continue in an old thought that brought pain and suffering into human life, because pain is thought to be inevitable? And the new metaphysics is better than the old philosophy of life. The old interpretation of life was hard put to it to explain why this good man suffered and that bad man went free. The new says, "Be he good or bad, he will suffer so long as his thought is wrong. Instead of believing that suffering is the inevitable 'chastening of the Lord,' let him perceive that it is the inevitable consequence of wrong-doing or of wrong thinking, and let him change his doing and his thinking and he will recover."

So let us realize that there is release from ills of flesh, because "flesh" is only the manifestation of our thought. The body is not "helpless" and "heir" to pain and fear and grief. Spirit is not bound save by the tangled threads of thought. Let us think and know the truth which makes us free. "Perfect God, perfect man, perfect body." "Be ye therefore perfect even as your Father in Heaven is perfect." Jesus was, in body and in mind and in character. So may we be.

REALIZATION.

I am conscious of my at-one-ment of nature with the Father. I know that God is all and that there is none other but He. Since He is all and yet "I am," therefore, "I and the Father are one." Since we are one I share his nature and resources. All that the Father hath is mine. My soul thrills with the wonder of it, my thought enlarges, I pass into deep experiences of joy in the revelation that is mine. *I* can, because God can. I know, because I am instructed by Him Who Knows. I cannot fail, because God fainteth not, neither is He weary. I wait on the Lord that He may renew my strength. I trust in the Lord and I am therefore as Mount Zion which cannot be moved but abideth forever. (Now take time to meditate on the

wonderful powers and possibilities open to you. Your
resources cannot fail. Failure is due to the fact that
you have not drawn upon God. Take what you will.
Ask and ye shall receive. Then meditate on the fact
that as you share the nature of God there is no mind
in the universe greater than the mind in you. Why
then should you cringe before the opinions of men?
Why should you walk in fear of criticism, tradition, or
prejudice of others?) I form my own opinions, I make
my own judgments, I set my own standards. I am a
man! I am a master of life! I do not try to tell others
how they *must* go. By my life I show them how they
may go. I am glad for this new freedom of consciousness. I am glad that I share the nature of God for this
means that I am eternal, I am indivisible from the
Father, I am truth, I am life, I am wisdom, in my
inner being. The inner man is perfect and day by day
I shall now show forth this perfection in my acts and
thoughts. I am a child of the Living God. And I am
glad.

LESSON VIII

MATTER, OR THOUGHT IN FORM.

WHAT we seek to do in this chapter is to show that the substance which we call "matter" is simply a grouping of particles* of energy or "electrons" and that these *electrons or energy are created by thought.* This can be shown by experiments that have been made with the mind of the individual, which reveal the fact that his thought either creates energy or puts it into purposeful activity. Then we want to show that the *form* things take is in response to a corresponding thought. When we understand that the material of which things are made is thought-energy or vibration and that it can be moulded into form by the thoughts we think, we are prepared to realize that the world we live in is very real and that what we need to do is not to deny it, but to understand it, in order to be masters of our bodies and conditions.

Physical science traces matter back to its origin in a primary substance which it calls ether. This ether pervades all space everywhere and there is no place where it cannot be found. Ether is simply a name given to that which can neither be seen, felt,

---

*Note. Technically the electron is not a "particle" but a property of matter.

tasted, nor actually examined scientifically, yet the
necessity of the case posits its omnipresence. It is a
frictionless, pulseless, motionless medium until it is
moved by some form of energy.

I. THOUGHT AND ENERGY OR MATTER.

When a visible universe comes into existence, it
begins with a movement of some sort within the invisible ether. Science speaks of the movement as the
activity of "vortex rings" or whirling particles of
energy which gradually coalesce into nebulæ or vapors;
and these violently throw out vast fragments into the
ether to congeal into planets and systems. Such activity can be seen even at this day in the nebulæ of
Andromeda where a new universe is in process of
creation.

Science therefore perceives that the visible universe
is composed of infinitely small particles of energy
called electrons. These electrons are the same kind
whether in a planet, the wood in a table, or the brains
in a man's head,—a fact which may seem highly un-
complimentary to the latter. The difference between
"substances" is then merely the difference in the num
ber of particles to a given area and the rate of their
motion.

These infinitely fine energized particles coalesce
sufficiently to form the various things which we
call mineral, animal, or vegetable substance. But
they never actually coalesce into an indivisible unit for
we discover that each atom of energy is separate from

every other and that indeed each is as widely separated from the other according to its size as the planets are according to their size and that there is a further similarity from the fact that each atom revolves upon its own axis. The "world of matter" therefore is really a world of energy and *so-called substance is vibration.* It is very important for the student to fix this in mind as the necessary basis of understanding the mental origin of the universe, and I would advise the reading of some book in elementary science or at least a free use of the Encyclopædia at this point as space forbids a further study here.

Since we live in a *world of energy,* since the sub stance of the universe is really energy, the problem of science and philosophy alike has been to account for the *first* presence of energy in ether. What force moved upon or within ether to give the vortex rings their first impulse? Many physical scientists now declare that the explanation is metaphysical or due to the act of a Will or Mind. The student may therefore wisely engage his attention in solving this problem.

ETHER AND COSMIC MIND.

The difficulty of explaining the origin of the universe is easily dissolved by the mental scientist who perceives in so-called "ether" merely another name for Cosmic Mind. The physical scientist's description of ether exactly corresponds with the mental scientist's explanation of Mind or Universal Creative Intelligence. The movement which results in electrons and vortex rings is the movement of the Divine Will within the Cosmic Mind; in other words, Mind thinks, and thinking creates energy, and energy in the form of electrons produces a universe.

What is now needed to make this clear is a scientific demonstration that *thought produces energy.* If we can show that the individual mind can produce energy or act upon it to cause its movement, we can better understand how the energy at the base of the universe was produced in the existing visible cosmos and is being produced in any universe now in the process of making. Many modern experiments in physical and psychic phenomena support the claim of the power of mind to produce energy.. Among them we might mention experiments by Sir William Crookes and Dr. Hippolyte Baraduc. The investigations of Sir William Crookes, many of them verified by other famous scientists and vouched for by the Society of Psychical Research and kindred scientific organizations, reveal that there is some power in the human body which he calls "psychic force" which goes forth to move ponderable bodies *at the will of the individual.* For example, he arranged a system of levers which when moved would cause a needle to register the movement automatically on a smoked-glass plate The operator then approached one end of the lever and without touching any part of the apparatus caused the lever to move, and the needle to make the record required. This experiment was repeated under varying conditions. This proves at least that thought produces sufficient energy to act upon material objects./ Nor can one object by saying that it is physical magnetism of the body rather than psychic; since if physical energy does flow out to cause the movement, still that energy was first moved by the mind of the operator./ Thought therefore produces energy. ✓

This is perhaps made still plainer by an experiment of Dr. Baraduc's, a popular account of which may be secured by the student in Judge Troward's Lectures on Mental Science.* Dr. Baraduc took a bell made of glass and suspended in it, by means of a silken thread, a copper needle. This he placed on a wooden base above the coil which was used to strengthen any energy transmitted to it, but which was not connected with a battery. Two bells are used in the experiment; and the operator holds his hands on either side, but not touching them. The copper needle is then found to move in response to the thought of the operator, a wide variance being found in the degree of movement according to the positive or negative nature of the mental attitude.

The value of this experiment is that it reveals that thought produces energy, for even if the needles were not moved directly by mental currents, still the mind had the power through thought to start a corresponding energy to moving through the body. The point of interest to us is that we learn from the foregoing experiments that *thought moves* and probably *creates energy*. Will acting on Creative Mind produces energy;

---

*Edinburgh Lectures on Mental Science. By T. Troward. Pages 108-111.

and this must be true whether the will be that of the Universal or the individual since in either case it acts on the same mind. *There is only one Creative Mind.* (See Lessons V and VI.)   This is made clearer when we think of ether as Universal Mind or the Ever-Present Intelligence.   This is the infinite repose or base of all things, the potential of things, but not everywhere active.   Since it is not everywhere active, energy is not found everywhere but only in places selected by Spirit for creative activity.   (See Lesson XXVIII.)   When the creation of a cosmos begins, a convulsive movement takes place in selected areas and the primary energy of a universe appears.   The universe in which we live, therefore, is to be conceived of as thought and the *whole existing cosmos as Mind in Action.*

The student should not fail to observe that we thus have great facts of mental science graphically proven to us.   The universe is created from some power resident within.   It is made out of Mind; or in other words, Spirit makes things by becoming the things which it makes.   Substance, in its last analysis, is intelligence.   Thought therefore turns into things.   "The Word is made flesh and dwells among us."   Since substance is intelligence, it is governed by intelligence. Since the foundation of the world is Mind, it must be *one*

This should clarify the thought of the student as to the part he may play in the Divine Plan, for if Spirit produces a world by becoming that world (see

"Being and Becoming" and "Creative Mind") then
we produce the thing we desire by becoming that
thing. Practically speaking, it means nothing less than
our ability to rule our world and by our thinking to
cause the things we desire to assemble themselves
about us. Carrying this to the ultimate of the power
inherent in us, it means that as Jesus materialized from
the atmosphere the bread and fish, so may the enlightened consciousness some day aspire to rule his
world. If we cannot today use the full power of the
sons of God, we can at least expect that our bodies
should yield to our will, our environment reflect our
mental attitudes, and material possessions come into
our hands. And to as many as receive, to them gives
He power to become the sons of God in very truth of
understanding. This is the truth which if known shall
make us free.

II. Thought and Form.

It now remains for us to show that *thought gives
form to substance,* a fact which is demonstrated
without difficulty once the foregoing principle is
known. As we have learned, creation is growth, unfoldment, or expansion of the "principle of life" from
within. That which we call life or intelligence, then,
first produces energy or vibration of which the visible
universe or cosmos is composed. On the other hand,
*the visible universe everywhere manifests itself in
form.* Since Mind is the primary power, since it
creates particles of energy and these particles of en-

ergy everywhere group themselves in form, only one conclusion is possible: **Thought Moulds Substance into Form.**

It is a principle inherent in Nature herself that substance should assume harmonious form. This is illustrated in the snow-flakes which fall in varied, flower-like patterns from the silent sky. Or one may study the tendency in an interesting experiment in musical vibration. Grains of sand sprinkled on a piece of plate glass, properly poised, will draw together into beautiful geometric figures when the bow of a violin is drawn across the edge of the glass, and each musical vibration will change the form the sand assumes.

Wonderful as are these experiments, they are scarcely comparable with a thousand unnoted miracles of creation about us. Examine the formative power of creative thought in an acorn. In that frail shell, a mighty oak lies cradled and an instinctive intelligence which will unfold its life into definite form.

Turn to the stars and study the inner tendency of all matter to coalesce, to rotate, and to assume spherical form; and then turn back to the other end of the creative scale and examine the development of human life. Within the fetus is the sleepless and mysterious intelligence which we call subconscious mind which produces the matchless and intricate mechanism some day to be in the form of man.

Do we not perceive, therefore, that *the substance of the invisible universe is mind: that thought produces*

energy or the substance of the visible universe by act-
ing upon the invisible: and again, that thought moulds
this energy or matter into form? *We are led, there-*
fore, to the inevitable conclusion that **the Existing**
Cosmos Is Thought in Form; that it exists and
moves in the limitless sea of the unmanifest Mind;
and that potential power lies in that Mind to create
new universes and new forms when and where It will.

Conclusions.

The student should carefully study and *learn* the
foregoing facts as the working basis of Mental Science. From them he may draw many conclusions. He
will perceive that he does not have to deny matter in
order to control bodies and conditions; he only needs
to recognize its nature as responsive intelligence. The
universe is real; matter is real; things are thoughts,
or, to be more accurate, are Mind taking form through
thought. We can control our world of interest because of the intelligence in it which is obedient to
thought, provided we are conscious of the facts we
have learned in the preceding chapters that in our
potential nature *we are one with the Infinite Creative*
Mind.

Finally, we should observe that the intelligence acts
on an *impersonal* basis, creating on the pattern which
our thought affords to it. It is entirely neutral; and we
may mould substance by our thought either into magnificent physical manhood and womanhood or into
deformed, emaciated and cancerous flesh. Our word

or thought is literally "made flesh and dwells among us." We get out of our universe what we put into it, for it reflects our moods and thoughts. (See Lesson XII, *et al*). Good and evil are alike real, *as effects,* but they are simply the outer expression of inner concepts. (See Lesson XVIII.) And you live in an eternal, undying universe, for though form and thought may change, the primary substance can never pass away. The primary substance is Mind, and as you share in It, you too are eternally at one with It. As the Infinite Responsive Intelligence, It is your Father leading you in green pastures and beside the still waters.

REALIZATION.

Study your universe to add your own conclusions to those already given. Study it to perceive the Ever-Present Good. Look for God in all and through all. Your power of understanding Him should be infinitely increased by this study. Your faith should be enlarged with these enlarged concepts of God. Let your realization be therefore one of thanksgiving.

I thank Thee, Father, that thou hearest me always. I thank thee that before I call Thou wilt answer me because Thou hearest my unspoken thought. I am conscious that my world reflects my moods and thoughts, and with that realization I will take care to think, speak, and hear only the beautiful, the good, and the true. I give Thee thanks that I can now see how "I and the Father are one," and I would ever press closer to Thee in the consciousness of the Divine Presence. I know that in this consciousness my thoughts will be right, my heart will be right, and therefore my universe will be right, since it reflects my thoughts and unspoken words. I am filled with joy and great peace; the joy of creative power, since "all power is given unto me in heaven and on earth"— the joy of Divine Fellowship with Thee, O Father, in all the eternal concerns of Thy kingdom. I thank Thee for the gift of life and eternal love. Amen.

LESSON IX.

THE CREATIVE WORD.

THE whole universe is alive with cosmic intelli gence; it is Infinite Creative Mind at work. As we have already seen, mind gives birth to thought and then uses its thought as the model of its creation, just as the artist conceives the idea of his picture and then uses the ingenuity of his brain and hand to picture forth its beauties in form and color. The mind, therefore, whether of the Universal or the Individual, has but *one* way to act at the beginning of any series; it must act by thought. And thought, in turn, always expresses in words. We always think in concrete terms or words. So we are told by John, "In the beginning was the Word, and the Word was with God and the Word was God. All things were made by Him and without Him there was not anything made that was made." And we are told in another place in Scripture, "By the word of the Lord were the heavens made, and all the host of them by the breath of His mouth." This is the answer to the question of science, "How did vibration originate?" It is easy enough to explain the evolution of the planetary systems and the life of the universe if we can explain the first introduction of motion, but whence did that come?

64

We learn from the study of physics that the nature of primal substance or ether is that all its particles are in perfect equilibrium or balance. The only way this balance can be disturbed and brought into form is by the application of some *immaterial* force to primal substance. We must therefore posit a Will somewhere, or the act of Mind, for that is the only possible immaterial force. So science may say that the "vortex ring" which is the first movement in the beginning of a universe takes its motion from the act of Mind. This is in harmony with what we have learned about Spirit, that "it is the power that makes things." The ancient seers knew this before science began; and they said, "The Spirit of God hath made me, and the Breath of the Almighty giveth me life."

Life can only come from Life, and motion can only have its origin in mind. The word spirit comes from the Latin, "spiro," "I breathe" The universe therefore springs from the out-breathing of Mind. This is the expansive movement of spirit with which ancient philosophers deal so much; as the Bible says, "The spirit of God moved on the face of the waters." The word "waters" is the esoteric term for Mind or Creative Mind. The Word acts on Mind to produce substance in the visible universe and then to bring that substance into varied forms, in sun, moon, stars, land, sea, vegetation, and man

So we find that Mind acts by thought, thought expresses in words, and we may go one step further and say that words are expressed by the voice. Therefore all ancient writers dealt much with the Voice. "The Voice of the Lord is upon many waters." The Sanskrit writings speak of Vach; the Latin is Vox, or Voice. In other words, the objective universe which is made up of motion or vibration in some form or other begins with the Voice. Until the Voice speaks the universe exists only in Creative Mind. As soon as Creative Mind selects a place to begin the creation of a universe, it then starts motion or vibration by the Voice. The whole objective world can be explained as vibration in some form or other. Everything from the gold in your watch to the light in the sun, from the chair you sit on to the brains in your head is composed of particles of substance at different rates of vibration. All material things can be divided into atoms, and theoretically dissolved into ether. Ether is simply another name for Mind. The electron is energy. The ultimate substance of which all things are made is the same therefore. But objects differ in the number of particles to a certain area and the rate of their motion. This is something we may all pause to meditate on because it *shows us that we live in a universe that is all one.* Says William Hayes Ward, "The whole great universe of starry worlds is one, built out of the same materials, moved by the same forces, governed by the same physical law. It is all one single system, one law, one order of thought, one scheme, one geometry, one plan fitted to one formula, one unitary universe."

This one substance is Mind, the one force is the force of thought which becomes concrete in words and expresses in Voice or vibration. For a voice is only intelligible vibration, or purposeful sound. Again the purposeful sound must be the Word.

We see, therefore, that the Creative Principle is the Word. "By the Word of the Lord were the heavens made."

OUR CREATIVE WORD.

We do not need to go further to draw the inference as to our own creative word. If we share the nature of God, if our thought acts on Original Substance, that is, in the Divine Mind; then every word *we* speak, whether we are shallow or deep, is a creative word. That is why we are told, "By thy words thou shalt be justified and by thy words thou shalt be condemned." Such is the fateful activity of the word we send forth into the universe. Something of the power and persistence of the words we speak may be gathered from a new and strange phenomenon discovered in the wireless telegraph instrument. It seems that operators keep picking up strange sounds, the apparent echoes of band music and so on. Many believe that the vibrations thus picked up may have started in the atmosphere long ago; how long no one knows. It is conceivable that the vibration started by the musical instrument, or the voice, may never die out. It is probable that it never does die. It enters the primary ether and sets it in motion; and nothing stops it from echoing forever. Perhaps some day the refined wireless instrument will be picking up out of the ether vast the words of the Master Teacher as he talked centuries ago by the Sea of Galilee to his companions or as he stood before Pilate or from the cross said, "Father, forgive them for they know not what they do."

However this may be, we may be sure of one thing, that *our* word is creative, that it acts on our conditions, our universe, and our own bodies. How careful then should we be in the selection of the things we are to say! We must let no word fall on some sensitive ear to rankle in some heart with its hurt, to act as suggestion to base thought, to draw men down.

>   "Let me no wrong or idle word
>   Unthinking say,
>   Set thou a seal upon my lips
>   Just for today."

How often men literally damn their home, their business, and themselves by the idle words they speak! To utter a pessimistic thought is to create an atmosphere to correspond (See Lesson XXVII) and thus to bring upon you the thing you fear. To speak unkindly to others is to curse them. To criticise is to push still further into the mire the one against whom your criticism is directed. "Every idle word that men shall speak, they shall give account thereof in the day of judgment." That day is now. The author knew of a woman recently whose idle tongue caused so much disturbance that it cost her husband one of the finest positions in his profession in the state. Her careless use of words destroyed his position.

On the other hand, the noble soul is always speaking constructive words, words of cheer, words of good-will, words of encouragement to all whom he meets. Such men are benefactors of their race, yet their service is one which any soul can render if he will. He blesses all mankind, but mankind in turn calls him blessed; and thus to boost others is to boost himself. Yet the noble soul does not think of this. He casts his bread on the waters but not that it may return in many days. Rather, he does it because he loves his fellowmen. His "word becomes a lamp unto the feet and a light unto the path."

If you would then become one of the helpers of your generation, fill your heart and thought with the best things. "Keep thy heart with all diligence for out of it proceed all the issues of life." Our words will come forth with beauty and grace as we have beauty and grace in our heart and thought.

> "Then let your secret thoughts be fair;
> They have a vital part and share
> In shaping words and moulding fate,
> God's system is so intricate."

REALIZATION.

I know that I control my world and my destiny by the thoughts I think. I know that if my heart is right, my thoughts will be right; if my thoughts are right, my words will be right; if my words are right, my world will be right. I therefore will set a seal upon my lips. I will guard my every thought and word. I will think no evil; I will hear no evil; I will speak no evil. I will set my mind on the highest things and the best. My tendency to speak critically is now gone from me; my habit of fault-finding is gone. I no longer damn myself, my friends, or my business by my words of pessimism. I am all optimism and hope, I am full of good cheer. I bless everybody and everything. I am an encouragement to all. "My word is made flesh and dwells in reality." Let me be ever filled with hope and cheer. Let the spirit of the Lord be on me. (Then realizing the creative power of your words, give the command to your conditions. Say, "Let this thing be done."- This is the creative word, the word of confident command. Let it be done unto me even as I will. *This* is my will.)

I thank Thee, Father, for this confidence and because Thou teachest me all things and givest me all things.

LESSON X.

THE OUTER AND THE INNER UNIVERSE.

THE imagination of man stands awed before the vastness of the universe in which he lives. He stands at night watching the stars prick forth into the infinite reaches of space. With his naked eye he can see 3,000. He goes to the telescope; and through the lens 100,000,000 pass across his startled vision. He places a photographic plate beneath the instrument and it records one million million.

Each of these stars is a sun and many of the suns are vaster than the great orb that makes our day. Beside these stars, he is told by science, there are as many more dead suns streaming in endless procession through space. Around each of these suns revolve various numbers of planets, just as the earth, Jupiter, Venus, Neptune and others revolve around ours. Our sun has eight planets. Some of the planets in turn have several moons revolving around them. Jupiter has eight. Dismayed by the very vastness, we are yet told by science that undoubtedly other suns and planets exist beyond the reach of any means that can be devised to detect them. Not only so, but new planetary systems are springing into being at this time. The nebulae of Andromeda are the first gatherings through

71

glowing gases of a new universe which some day will
be flung in glorious constellation across the ethers.

Numerous as are these stars, yet they do not jostle
each other in space. Our own sun, which is a star to
other planets, is 93,000,000 miles from the earth and
is traveling at the rate of 800 miles a minute. The
next nearest star, Alpha Centaura, is distant about
25,000,000,000,000 miles. The North star circles the
heavens 316,666,666,000,000 miles away

Light travelling at the rate of 186,000 miles per
second requires years to reach our planet. Science
shows us that it takes the light of some of the nebulae
8,000,000 years to come to us.

No eye really has ever beheld a star. We have only
seen the light which has been streaming from it for
perhaps millions of years.

Vast as are these distances, they are matched by a
peerless harmony that holds all the stars in fixed and
definite orbits. By a mutual attraction and repulsion,
they make their own untroubled way through the invisible pathways of the sky.

Our very imagination is for a moment overwhelmed
with the thought of a universe at once so vast and so
harmonious. Freely the stars swing out into space,
yet move under fixed laws and in rhythm so perfect
that many people believe, and with reason, in the very
music of the spheres.

Yet the awful majesty of the heavens, the infinite
evolution of the planets has found its equal in the
matchless mind of man. For all that is evolved out

there is involved in me here. I have in me something that mates it at every point. I could not grasp it, I could not recognize it, unless there were in me a consciousness as great as the heavens. In me is a something which we call mind that can "take in" the whole starry vault. I can gather it all into my own mind. I can recognize it. I can swallow it all in a glance. There must therefore be involved in me all that is evolved out there.

REALIZATION.

I have in me the vast universe of thought. I, looking at the stars, am greater than the stars looking at me. They find in me the matchless capacity to understand them. I am above them for I am conscious of both them and myself. I am made as the angels of heaven. I tread upon the pathway of the stars. I move amid the eternal ways as master. By my mind I am king of the worlds. Today I go about my work with the step of a monarch. Am not I one with the power that made the spheres, since I am greater than they? I am. Today I will live above fear, and smallness, and meaness of any kind. I will companion with stars. I will rest in the quiet confidence that He who brought these into being and holds the heavens in his hand, shall keep me in perfect security—for I am one with the Mind that made them.

THE INFINITE SELF.

OUR ability to conceive of God in his infinite qualities requires an inherent infinite capacity in ourselves, as we saw in the lesson on the Outer and Inner
Universe in the previous chapter. Today we want
to study the attributes of the Infinite which are
infinite in the self. We must realize that while we
never *express* all of them in their entirety at any
time, yet they exist as the background of our life and
the possibilities of our being. The volume of water
in a canal may be limited at any given moment, yet
back of it and at one with it lies the ocean from which
it can limitlessly draw. We have attributes of being
co-extensive with Spirit or God himself. These are
love, life, and wisdom.

Love in us is infinite, for no one ever did or ever
can exhaust the supply of love in himself. Indeed, the
more we love, the more we feel the power within us
of further loving. The noblest cosmic soul, instead of
exhausting his resources of love, becomes rather a
type of the

> "Immortal love, forever full,
> Forever flowing free,
> Forever shared, forever whole,
> A never-ending sea."

74

Life in us is also infinite. However fully we live, we have but an increasing sense of our own livingness. Much health begets more; and he who most truly lives, most surely believes in exhaustless energies behind. It is only the invalid who loses faith in the boundless life and the weakling that fears its end. Life cannot be "lived up," for it is infinite.

Wisdom, too, is infinite. No one has ever exhausted his capacity to think new thoughts and utter new sayings. The greatest scholars have always recognized that whatever knowledge they have expressed and truths they have outlined are as nothing compared with the number of those yet to be brought forth out of the mind.

We may say then that in the essential attributes of godhood—love, life, and wisdom—man is infinite in potential quality. We can now go a step further and say that this life, love, and wisdom is that of God himself. The logic is simple. These powers are infinite. There cannot be *two* infinites of the same kind. But these are of the same kind, for if they were not, we would not be able to understand them in God for we would have no way of feeling any sense of relationship with them. We can be conscious of anything only as we feel some relationship to it. Since, then, these attributes of life, love and wisdom in God are the same kind as our own, and since both are infinite, they *must be one.* Jesus knew it.

The Master Teacher exclaimed, "I and the Father are one." And they took up stones to stone him.

"Many good works have I shown you from the Father; for which of those do ye stone me?" he asked.

"For a good work we stone thee not, but for blasphemy; and because that thou, being a man, makest thyself God."

"Is it not written in your law: 'I said, ye are gods?'"

Looking into the faces of those whose hate, hypocrisy, and legal power sought to destroy him, Jesus proclaimed the divinity of man. "If I do not the works of the Father, believe me not. But if I do them, though ye believe not me, believe the works; that ye may know and understand that the Father is in me, and I in the Father." And later he said two significant things of those who were to follow him, "Greater works than these shall ye do because I go unto the Father," and, "That they may be one even as we are one."

If the "works" men do are the test of divinity and "greater works" are now being done, may we not say that man's divinity is today being more highly attested than ever before? And these works must be ever greater as you come more and more to understand the *infinite resources of the self;* for, as you learn in the lesson on the law of correspondences, you manifest or externalize (this mean, "the work") just what you think within. Your power to control the conditions of your life depends entirely on your ability to comprehend in larger measure the truth of your own inherent and infinite life, love, and wisdom. As your ideas grow, so will your capacity increase to embody them, faith in form, until at last you stand master of fate.

REALIZATION.

Meditate on the truth just expressed. It is merely a sketch; you can fill in the outline with your own meditation. Bring your thought up to a high point by "imaging" and "feeling" the vastness of this God Power in you—the Infinite Self. If infinite, it can never be exhausted, never fail, never die. Think of it! "I and the Father are one." All day you are in the Presence of the Infinite. Practice that Presence to-day. Read Chapter ten, verses 19 to 38 in John. Learn a few of the best verses. Learn the four-line stanza of "Immortal Love." Fill your mind with the truth and then say:

I am living today the infinite life; therefore am I *perfectly* well. I am loving with an infinite love, therefore am I *perfectly* happy; I am thinking with the mind of infinite wisdom, therefore I have peace and harmony. Today I have peace, poise, and a feeling of power. I am living in the life, love, and wisdom of the Infinite. So be it!

LESSON XII.

THE LAW OF ATTRACTION AND APPROPRIATION.

OUR gifts from heaven are those only which we will receive. We must learn that we can receive from the Law only what we give to the Law; that the Law assumes toward us just the attitude we assume toward it. If we conceive of God as a loving Father, he becomes that to us and comes out with open arms to welcome his loved one home. If, on the other hand, we see in Him only a stern and relentless judge, we find the Law reacting to us relentlessly. If, further, we look upon the Law as our antagonist, that it becomes to us, and is the "adversary" of which Jesus spoke who will "not let us go until we have paid the utmost farthing." We can conceive of the Law as a magic mirror which creates in form and substance just what we reflect into it. Infinitely exact and creative, it takes the loveliest reflection of face and form and makes it into a breathing thing of flesh. Or it takes the hideous face like that of the Medusa and it becomes a living creature with its writhing locks of serpents. But this magic mirror reflects that which is more subtle than flesh; it catches the vision of our thoughts; it takes the imaginations of our heart, and breathes them into life and form. So the loveliest thought draws forth its own sweet self clothed in flesh; and base thought and passion are moulded into deeds

78

and acts as vile. Why? Because the universe assumes to us just the attitude we take toward it. This is what we call the law of correspondences.

From this it becomes evident that what we receive from the Law depends on our ability to conceive. How much faith have you? The Law will justify it. Can you conceive of the Infinite Good as ready to pour out for you above all you ask—with the universal plus added to it? "According to your faith it will be done unto you." "Give unto the Law, and it shall be given unto you; good measure, pressed down and running over shall be given into your bosom." "Ask and ye shall receive; seek and ye shall find; knock and it shall be opened unto you." "If a son asks bread, will he (the father) give him a stone, or fish and he give him a serpent?" "How much more then will your Heavenly Father give good gifts to them that ask him!"

We note here that Jesus shows the exactness of the law; if you expect bread, you will get bread, if fish, you will get fish. And if you expect a stone, you will get it. Our bread from heaven comes then in response to the attitude we mentally assume toward heaven, so that it becomes plain that the thing we need to do is to grow a deeper consciousness or capacity to conceive and appropriate. Let us today look upon our universe with faith, faith in all nature, faith in man, faith in God.

REALIZATION.

I look for the good and the good only. I see the

good in everything and everybody. God is Good and He gives to me above all I ask or think. I see in Him my loving Father, my gracious Redeemer. I perceive the harmony in all things, and the beneficent mind of the Universe. God is Father of all, and therefore I behold in everyone my friend and brother. No man's hand is set against me; and my hand is not set against anyone. All men everywhere are my kindred, and I am a friend to all. Beholding the infinite response of nature, man and God to my mood, I am today thinking only high and fine thoughts. I am filled with the brightest and finest faith and emotions. (Now take up the thought of healing for body or conditions. Think how the sickness is due to wrong thinking somewhere. Find out if you can the mental cause that produced it, and mentally or physically cast it into outer darkness—which is to recognize that it has no power over you and is therefore nothing to you.)

The only power this has I have given to it. I now withdraw the power, which is my belief in this evil; and it falls into elemental nothingness. I am now full of faith in my healing. I am a child of Spirit—perfect and complete. My thoughts are thoughts of health and harmony. I now receive health and harmony; Creative Mind is working to create for me a perfect correspondent to my thought. My thought is perfect, my faith is sure. I have a perfect concept of health. Today I am healed. I thank Thee, Father, that thou hearest me always. Today I talk with Thee and walk with Thee; I am sure of myself and Thee and All. So be it.

LESSON XIII.

CHOOSING THE LAW YOU WILL LIVE UNDER.

EACH of us selects the law under which he will live. It is not true that we make the law; but we decide which law we will obey. The citizen lives under the civil law which he has helped to make. If he did not make it, still he elects to live under it, for he can emigrate to another country or he can refuse to obey it. The soldier puts himself under the military law and the sailor submits himself to the law of the sea. The physician subjects himself to the law of medicine, and the osteopath to the law of manipulation. The fearful trembling soul elects to live under the law of chance and finds himself in a world that corresponds, with accidents, floods, and sudden storms. The drug fiend, the drunkard, are ruled by the law of their choice, preferring its hard tasks rather than the surrender of its sensations. The pessimist chooses to live under the law of the cloud; and the optimist under the law of the sun. The materialist lives in a world of matter governed by material laws and in a universe of fatalism. The glorified soul says, "I live in a world of mind and will obey its laws. I have my being in a world of spirit and can control my own conditions. I exist in the heart of the Infinite and will enjoy Its fruits of love, for the fruits of the Spirit are love, joy, and peace."

What law are you living under today? You may choose which one. But remember that within each law the fundamental principle of the universe is still at work; every cause will have its effect. Every good deed has its reward; every evil word has its consequences; every act of faith will draw its high behest from heaven.

Today, therefore, let me choose to live under the highest law of being, and let me go on in perfect security. If I keep my law, my law will keep me. If I obey my law, my law will obey me. Let me not forget that I make my world by the thoughts I think.

REALIZATION.

My law today is love, faith, prosperity and truth. I look unfalteringly into the future for I am today sowing the seed for my future harvest, and it is good. I expect a good harvest. So today I rest in peace and faith. I trust in God. His law is love.

LESSON XIV.

FEELING AND EMOTIONS.

IN feeling is the creative power; and there is the real divinity of man. One's first impression is that it lies in thought. But deeper than thought is the power that produces it and the feeling that creates it. We think because we feel. Creation is not directly in thought but in feeling. Every word we speak is a creative word, but it is the feeling that it expresses and which accompanies it that creates. The deepest feeling produces the highest creation. A word spoken in love produces harmony in body and ease in conditions. A word spoken in hate throws poison into the blood and produces physical discord for the hater. This is the more easily understood when we think of the creative mind in terms of subjective mind. This mind is the seat of all emotions and feelings; the objective mind has only memories of the emotions that have been experienced. The subjective mind is simply another name for creative mind; and therefore the creative mind acts on the feeling which in essence it is.

That all creative acts are accompanied by the highest feeling identifies feeling with the power to create. The union of the masculine and feminine principle is a lofty emotion whether it be in the mad affinity of the atoms, or the sweet fertilization of the plant or the procreation of animal life. Yet, as all acts on the sense plane are but the outer manifestation of an inner thought or feeling, and as all acts which are true to Nature are also true to God, the joy of physical creation is but the reflex or externalization of inner and finer feelings and emotions. The sense act is divine as all nature is divine from planet to man, since both are the product of Divine Mind, yet back of it lies the noble emotion of the soul,—the spiritual emotion. No feeling on the physical plane can rival the joy of mental creation as in the work of the inventor, artist, or composer. Yet above this shines the higher star of spiritual conception which is love. To express love is to outrival all the mad ecstasies of nature in the sweet ecstasy of the soul. Both can be defined as the union of kindred things, but love is the union of spirit with spirit, where soul meets soul and is satisfied. Love is the desire of God for completeness in another. This is Creative Feeling. It is to accomplish it that the whole universe is produced, that at the end of the series man might rise and *on his own initiative* seek completeness in God and thus enable God to fulfill his desire. Man thus pours back to God across the chords of life the rich music of a heart in tune with Him. Thus God and man and nature join in the great divine harmony of being. Feeling must be regarded, therefore, as the Divine-Power-to-Become Manifest. In the physical organism it is the genuine correspondent of the highest in spiritual being, and it exists in man as the basis of creative energy. Rightly directed, feeling can be depended on as the current of divine life flowing out into expression in all our affairs, in health and wisdom.

Do not fear the emotions, nor think there is virtue in the denial of the higher senses. That is a false philosophy. Rightly control the feeling, yet recognize it as Spirit's joy seeking expression through you. Deep feeling of genuine emotions of love, faith, sympathy, joy of existence, these are the creative factors, the positive elements in the realization of the new life. Abstract thinking, calm reasoning have no such power as *thought sustained* by feeling. Many people become intellectually persuaded of the truth of the new wave of life, which we call the science of mind, who yet do not get results through their knowledge. What is needed therefore is to bathe knowledge in the *deep feeling* of truth. How shall this be accomplished?

We must realize that it is secured in the same way as any other quality we desire. If we wish to develop a quality or demonstrate health or wealth, we do so by stating to ourselves that it exists, exists for us now, and by laying claim upon it. Then we go quietly about our work and expect the law to work out our manifestation for us. Mind then acts to produce in expression or form what we have given it in thought. The great moving heart of the universe stands ready to pour through the channels we provide, the life and love which It is. For us to recognize It is to allow It to become manifest for us. It assumes toward us the attitude we assume toward it. Knowing this, we may well put our knowledge into action through the following simple breathing exercise. All the finer forces of the body can be made to tingle with this exercise. Having found a restful position, breathe deeply and as you inhale, say, "I am breathing in all the love and faith of God. The spirit of life is now filling my whole body." Then, as you exhale, imagine yourself as diffusing all the new energy of life throughout the body and say, "I feel the presence of divine life passing through my whole being." This will produce a fine ecstasy as the thought at once puts the body into a vibration corresponding to it. This gives us feeling in physical expression which produces confidence that we can have mental and spiritual feel ing as well. In fact, we shall find that we do at once begin to feel the power of divine life in us. This exercise is especially desirable for those who, through over-effort of body or mind, have depleted what is often termed the "reserve power" and produced a condition of exhaustion. We are now ready to use the following meditation, striving always to feel as deeply as we can.

REALIZATION.

I know that God is life, love, and wisdom. I know that this life, love, and wisdom is in me for I am one with the Father. I know that in me is a vast power of faith. I feel the new confidence of one who draws from the heart of Infinite Love. "He that believeth on me, from within him shall flow streams of living water", said Jesus of the spirit. Love is in me, over me, around me, and through me. All power and love is given unto me. I am now receptive to the highest that God can give. I receive it in deepest joy and thanksgiving. I thank Thee, Father, that Thou hearest me always.

LESSON XV.

THE INSTINCT TO CREATE.

THE instinct to create is found in every normal person. It is one of the first tendencies of our childhood and persists so long as life holds any value for us. Being native to us all, it indicates a common source—it springs out of the Creative Mind Itself. Spirit is instinctively creative. God has creative desires and powers which can only be satisfied in making something. He longs to express his power to create, to use his thought to body forth his ideas into form. It is the passing of ideas out into form that produces joy and feeling of pleasure. God is the Great Artist who dreams a picture and then paints it; the Great Composer who feels his harmony within and seeks to voice it. He puts into form what he feels and thinks within.

We find the same thing to be true of ourselves. We are not all artists or musicians; but we all have creative instincts and the desire to make things. A woman likes to make a new hat and enjoys both the new creation and the admiration of her friends. She likes to stir up a cake and produce either a new recipe or get unusual results from an old one. She enjoys her home-making and the use of her mind in working for the church, charity, or the club. A man likes to

measure his mind against circumstances and the business world, to see what he can do with the materials
he has to work with, to devise new methods to meet
changing conditions, new forms of advertising or
economy, and to make an old business pay more.

Life has meaning and value only as we are able to
express our ideas and to create. When I was a young
man, I thought that only youth had its visions and its
dreams, and I said to a woman of forty, "I don't see
what there is in life for anyone who has reached your
age." "Oh, we have things we want to work out just
as you do," she said. She was full of creative ideas
and she joyed to bring them forth into form.

The reason why men and women "pass the dead
line" is because they have ceased to have creative
ideas and the desire to express them. So long as we
have interest, eagerness, enthusiasm and the desire to
create, we have something the world wants; and we
cannot pass the "dead line." Age lies not in years but
in feeling. To remain young, we must feel a desire to
act creatively.

People who are placed in a position where they
cannot express themselves are often crazed, or discouraged, or impoverished by their inability to create.
They can be healed by giving them something to do,
by finding new interests for them. Often shock, following the loss of a friend, paralyzes the creative instinct; and the cure lies in finding something helpful to
do, especially for those in great need. Often, too, one
may be helped by taking care of children, or in seeking

to make them happy and by watching them in their creative activity: to give a child a good time is to give one to yourself because you live again in the child. The life of a grandparent is happier than that of old age without children on this account.

Happiness, therefore, rises out of the joy of self-expression and in creative activity. If you are not happy, then look to your sources. Begin to think creative thoughts; seek creative ideas and impulses, demand opportunities to bring out into form all that you feel yourself to be. In the end, you will find that God is seeking self-expression in life, love, wisdom and form *in you.* Make yourself a channel for the highest and best that spirit has to utter through you. Creative Mind and you are *one.*

TREATMENT.

I am one with Creative Mind. It seeks in me its full expression. My joy is great that I am thus allowed to work with God. I am now filled with creative ideas and plans. I am one with All Wisdom that produces them. I am taught by spirit what things to think and do. I am lead by spirit to act wisely and truly today. I shall walk only in the paths of peace and power. I feel new powers and new capacity. I am renewed in mind and body. I thrill with joy and anticipation. I am conscious of the Presence of All Wisdom and Truth; and I am perfect success today.

LESSON XVI.

OUR IMMACULATE CONCEPTIONS.

WE are what we think. Our highest ideals control our interest and thus our thinking. Men's ideals are their religion for we cannot see God, but we can conceive of Him. The higher our ideals, therefore, the higher is our concept of God and the purer is our religion. Ideals and faith are blended into one. Our ideals are what we conceive of as possible; our faith is our belief that these ideals not only can but will be realized. The noblest manhood and womanhood becomes, therefore, the best exponent of Christianity; and to live nobly is to be a Christian in the truest sense.

The reason why we need to have high ideals is that the law creates for us on the model we give it. If our ideal of perfection is brute strength, *that* develops without the charm of personality and character. If, on the other hand, we think only of personality and social graces, *that* develops without adequate physical basis.

If our concept of wealth is that we can have just enough to pay the rent and the butcher, we develop capacity enough to earn just that. If, however, we can think of ourselves as living in a mansion and having all we may desire, then we find the law of correspondences working to give those to us. If we think we are governed by chance, war-conditions, and

competition, then *that* becomes our law. **If, again,**
we conceive of ourselves as above conditions, unlimited and absolute, then *that* becomes a fact to us.
Why?

All this is true because the Law assumes toward us
just the attitude we assume toward it. If then our
highest ideal and faith is that we are sons of God,
sharing his nature and resources, we have the basis
for the highest gifts from the Law because we dare to
conceive more for ourselves. A son has more faith in
prosperity and his future than a servant.

Our highest concept, therefore, is our vision of the
self as at one with the Father in nature and power,——
"I and the Father are one." So writes the Psalmist, "I
will lift up mine eyes unto the hills from whence
cometh my help; my help cometh from the Lord."
This is plainly the attitude to be assumed by one who
himself seeks to become an inspiration and an uplift
to mankind. He cannot lift up until he first be uplifted. He must first look to the heights, who would
point out to others the way. He must know the trail
in the ranges. He must himself stand on a summit.
He must have been on the Mount of Transfiguration.
The uplook must precede the uplift. One must know
the law, to teach it; the way, to show it; God, to reveal
Him. There must be an alliance with the Unseen. Out
of the hills comes help; from snow-capped mounts, the
cooling breeze; from forest glades, the notes of peace;
from rugged peaks, a faith sublime.   "The strength
of the hills is his also." The alliance with the Unseen

must never be forgotten. Where there is no inlet, there is no outlet. There is no river without a source, no stream without a rising spring. The fountain will not spray without the water. The ship will not sail without a breeze. Silent is the wheel without the belt; powerless the car without the current; dead is the lamp without the light. But linked with the source, the river runs, the fountain sprays, the ship sails, the wheel turns and "the lamp giveth light unto all who are in the house." We must look up, move up, reach up, and then we shall be prepared to lift up. We must be in alliance with the Unseen. In that day shall supernal forces seize us, possess us, sway us, use us. Then, having become the inlet, we shall also become the outlet of all there is in God. In that day the power of God will be revealed; "the blind will receive their sight, and the lame will walk; the leper will be cleansed, the poor will have the gospel preached to them; and blessed shall be he who shall not be offended in us." These shall be the signs following them that believe. But first there must be alliance with the Unseen—only the uplifted become an uplift!

Thus, to conceive of ourselves as at one with the Father is to endow us with "power from on high."

Let us not forget the reason why. The Law gives back to us *created,* what we think into it as *vision.* Let our visions therefore be high and true! Let them be glorified! And let us not forget that this is as true whether our ideals be for a perfect character, a perfect body, perfect wisdom in our business, or perfect

happiness. What do you want? *Picture* it as yours
now. Dream it into beauty. See it as you would have
it. The more perfect your vision, the more perfect
your returns. The perfect vision of faith is the im-
maculate conception of the pure mind. The Law, with
infinite intelligence, will body the faith into form.
Give yourself in faith to the highest visioning of your
soul.

"O young mariner,
　　Down to the haven
Call your companions,
　　Launch your vessel,
And crowd your canvas
　　And ere it vanishes
Over the margin,
After it, follow it,
　Follow the gleam!"

REALIZATION.

I am in Alliance with the Unseen. I am one with
the Father. All that the Father hath is mine. God is
my light and my salvation. I lift up mine eyes unto
the hills from whence my help cometh. My help
cometh from the Lord which made heaven and earth.
The strength of the hills is mine also. I am son of
God; I am heir to all that is. God is All-Power; therefore I have strength. God is All-Wisdom; therefore
I am guided in all my affairs. God is All-Supply;
therefore I shall not want. God is All-Love, therefore

I am filled with the highest love and affection. I cannot have a desire but God supplies it. His eye is on the sparrow; and I know He cares for me. I am completely satisfied in my consciousness of the Indwelling Presence. I will fear no evil for Thou art with me. Always and forever I am supplied. (In this high consciousness, conceive of the good you desire and hold it up to the Creative Mind and expect it to come into you. Hold it in consciousness for a while. Feel it deeply. I do believe. I am satisfied. Conclude by saying the Lord's prayer with deep feeling and thought. You thus get down into Creative Feeling. Let it be done unto you. Now give thanks.) It is done. "I thank Thee, Father, that Thou hearest me always."

LESSON XVII.

INTENSIFIED CONSCIOUSNESS.

CONSCIOUSNESS of truth is the great goal of the metaphysician. He must have a deep-seated perception of reality or his word is unbacked by power. His consciousness is the weapon with which he puts to flight the whole evil array of wrong thoughts, wrong concepts, and fears with all their attendant diseases and limitations. It is his shield against doubt and discord. It is the standard around which he rallies all the forces of good and God. Sword and shield and standard, consciousness is simply *knowing in your heart* that all is good, all is God, and that your word is the word of authority to the Law. It is what the centurion recognized in Jesus when he said, "Sir, I am not worthy that thou shouldst come under my roof; but only *say the word* and my servant shall be healed. For I also am a man under authority, having under myself soldiers: and I say to this one, 'Go,' and he goeth; and to another, 'Come,' and he cometh; and to my servant, 'Do this,' and he doeth it." Without fully understanding it, the centurion voiced the law of consciousness. You must recognize that the Law is your servant and you must *feel* that when you speak the word, it will obey you; even more, that it has obeyed you.

This consciousness is not merely intellectual knowledge of the Law; it is far more than that; it is the *feeling* of truth. "As a man thinketh **in his heart** so is he." Every means, therefore, that can be employed to intensify this consciousness should be eagerly sought. And nothing is more desirable than a whole-souled, hearty commitment of oneself to truth. We may liken life to men in boats. One clings to the shore and his vessel breaks to pieces on the rocks. One sails up and down in the harbor, catching an occasional helpful breeze in his canvas as he steers for different points and arrives at length—nowhere, or else merely at the point of departure. One commits himself to God and the sea, and sets his sail and drives before the favoring winds to the island of treasures. A thorough commitment to the new way is absolutely essential. A half truth is often a whole lie; and a timid advance is the forerunner of defeat. Says Goethe,

"Thus indecision brings its own delays,
And days are lost, tormenting over days."

The more passionately you commit yourself to the highway of health, the more boldly you sail the sea of faith, the more certain are you of success. Jesus says, "From the days of John the Baptist until now the Kingdom of Heaven suffereth violence, and the violent take it by storm." The eager and enthusiastic followers of truth seize the Kingdom—win it as a prize of war.

Such a bold, violent commitment to the new way of faith is essential to the great progress of the soul. It is thus out of tempestuous abandonment that we get the rock-like Peter; the strong-souled St. Augustine; the towering Luther; the enthusiastic Wesley. Thus do we get our Caesars, plunging into the Danube to be baptized into kingship; our Cromwells to sit on thrones; our Washingtons to create nations; our Grants to save the causes of the people.

What is true here is true of the way of healing. "Commit thy ways unto the Lord, trust also in Him; and He shall bring it to pass." This is the supreme test, the indispensable condition of success, that one place the matter entirely on the plane of faith. Believe! Believe! Believe! Feel deeply! Know! "Knowledge is power." When you feel so deeply that you know, and know you know, then at that moment you are half way up the heights. In a little while you will stand at the summit. You are well and it is a godlike wellness. There is no danger of a relapse. Emblazon on the shield of your soul this one word, "Credo," I believe. You need no other motto.

THE REASONS FOR FAITH.

We always attempt to explain as clearly as we can not only the fact but the process. Why is faith essential to success? If you will examine with us for a moment a phenomenon of hypnotism you will clearly see the reason for faith. Of course this is illustrative only. Hypnotism is an inferior form of mental activity and should never be confounded with the higher forces of mental and spiritual methods of healing. In hypnotism the objective mind sleeps, in spiritual healing the mind is awake. But herein we find a good illustration furnished by the well-known educator, Dr. G. Stanley Hall. Take a long gas pipe from which project fifty lighted jets. Then turn out the lights one by one. The lights that remain burn all the more brilliantly, and the last jet blazes with a powerful radiance. A hypnotized man represents the same principle. A part of his mental and physical forces are shut off or put to sleep. Upon suggestion *of the operator* he now centers all his vital forces on one part of the body. He feels with greater intensity; he hears as no others present can hear; he remembers with startling accuracy. Tell him that a fire burns on his skin, he is in an agony of pain. Nor is this imagination. Blood and nerves actually respond to these suggestions. On awakening the patient recalls and performs orders given him in hypnotic sleep. But the point to note is the illustration of the centered thought, the *intensity of feeling.*

In the deep feeling of a perfect faith all the mental and bodily energies center on the focal point of the disease. Every blood vessel, nerve and energy of the body plies about the affected part with concerted zeal. A very torrent of activity may be thought of as going on there. On the mental model, the forces build. Each little workman says, "Brother, be of good cheer"; and they "help every one his neighbor." So the revitalizing, renewing, recreative processes go on. It is truth, therefore, that there is no disease but can be healed by the powerful emotions of a perfect faith.

Organic disease, we are told, cannot be cured. "Medical science and God stand abashed in its presence. God is able to heal functional disease but not organic." Cast this thought from your mind. "With God," said Jesus, *"all* things are possible." When medical science has reached its utmost limit, you may find "that man's extremity is God's opportunity." "Trust also in Him; and He will bring it to pass." Make your extremity God's opportunity by the intensity of your faith. Do not try by will-power to cause the structure of your body to change, or function in a different way. This is auto-suggestion. It is not powerful enough. Throw yourself on God. Declare your positive faith in God. Intensify it. Storm the throne of God. The violent take the Kingdom of heaven by storm. Have a passionate faith. The woman of Jesus' parable by her importunity prevailed over the judge. The man by his importunity secured the loaves of bread at the midnight hour. When the deep shadows of gathering darkness fall upon you, remember this: You can by persistent intensity secure the coveted good. And note this, that such faith is of greater value to soul than to body and that therefore you are not asking contrary to the will of God but in harmony with his plan.

> "Go on, true soul,
> You'll win the prize,
> You'll reach the goal."

REALIZATION.

"The Lord is my light and my salvation, Whom then shall I fear? The Lord is the strength of my life, Of whom shall I be afraid?"

I can pass through no experience where Spirit is not with me. I can have no accident when Spirit protects me. I can have no sorrow that Spirit cannot comfort me. I am kept in a serene and perfect love. I am held in the Mind of God. I cannot be lost, for there is no place outside of Divine Mind. I am surrounded by All-Good. I am embraced by All-Good. I am conscious of All-Good. All around me, in me, and through me is the Love that will not let me go. Though I walk in the shadows, He will be my light. Though I sail upon the sea, He will be my compass. Though I be alone, He will be my companion. Whom, then, shall I fear? I shall fear nothing and no one. Death can be no more, for the soul that knows that life is all. I can walk in the valley of the shadow, but life walks with me. I fear no evil. I am life; God is Life; all is Life; and I go on in faith and confidence.

LESSON XVIII.

IS EVIL A POWER?

"God is all in all"

THIS is the philosophy fundamental to Christian Healing. This is the healer's confidence. This is the truth whose realization is most essential to the acquirement of health. We must know that the eternal substratum of the universe is not material but spiritual, not temporal, but eternal. At the foundation is God. As the plant can never grow unless in the seed is the germ of life, in the sap is the principle of existence, so the universe must have at its heart the living presence of the eternal spirit. As the Apostle Paul says, "All must be subject to him that God may be all in all." As the poet has said, God is

"Above all things, below all things,
Within all things, around all things,
Within all, but not shut in,
Around all, but not shut out.
Above all as Revealer,
Below all as Sustainer,
Within all as newness of life."

This is above Pantheism, because it not only identifies God with the universe but it proves Him to be more than His universe. Again "God is love," therefore He must have an object of His affection, so that man, too, has an individual part in God, as this object of affection. God has personal attributes because He is conscious of Himself as loving and directing His power to beneficent ends.

How wonderful and significant this is! There is nothing but the divine presence everywhere, there is no real power except that of God. There is only one world; it is God's world. The only real world is the world that exists in the mind of God and in the mind of the individual. We live in a spiritual universe in which God is supreme.

This means, of course, that there is no real power opposed to God. Jesus voiced this truth in many ways. He quoted the commandment, "Hear, O Israel, the Lord thy God, the Lord is One" The pain and sickness and distress and want of the "little flock" were not due to the power of some evil force, but to the thralldom of fear and worry. Remove these things, and at once the law of good would operate for men as for the lilies of the field. It was not one power—the Power of Good—contending with another—the Power of Evil. It was the elimination, the annihilation of a mental mood, that was to open the way for God's sunshine to fall.

This then is the simple philosophy fundamental to this system of thought, recognition of which does so much to open up the way to health and peace and supply of every kind. *The only power is the God-power.* There is no real power to wrong or pain in themselves. Truth is the only reality. Evil has only so much power as we attribute to it. With Jesus we may affirm that Satan has no part in us.

Thus as darkness is legislated out of existence by the introduction of light, so evil is reduced to zero by the presence of the contrary thought. All this is in harmony with what we have learned about the Law, that man makes his own universe by his thinking; for the creative substance is plastic to his thought and takes the form and quality which his thought gives to it. (Lesson VII.) The original substance is without **qualities** of its own, being merely electronic energy, which is simply force created by the activity of the Divine Will. It is like the wax that awaits the imprint of the die or the marble that has not been chiseled upon by the hand and mind of the sculptor. But original substance is moulded into form and takes character through the most subtle of instruments, the thought of our mind. It becomes to us just what we think into it, just as the mirror takes on the form and color we give to it. If, therefore, we think limitation, we get its reflection in the lack of things; if we think supply, we get that. "As a man thinketh in his heart, so is he" in his *person.*

What Evil Means.

It is seen accordingly that evil lies in the consciousness and there it lies and lies. "But just what do we mean by evil?" is now a natural question. When we use the word "evil" of objective experiences, we refer to "physical evil" such as hardship, pain, poverty, unpleasant surroundings. When we use it of thought, we refer to mental attitudes and experiences which are due to wrong concepts and choices of the will. This latter is called by the theologians, "moral evil," and they say it is "some impulse or suggestion that was not worthy to be acted upon but was acted upon by beings who had the power to do otherwise. . .Sin first came by the act of created free spirits willing wrongly." (Christian Theology, page 155, Wm. N. Clarke.)

But the theologian fails to perceive two significant facts: first, that the choice of the impulse or suggestion is not due to wilful wickedness but to ignorance, since no one would make choices involving suffering and loss if he fully realized and felt the force of the disasters that follow upon them. This ignorance of action would be avoided by depending upon the intuitive guidance of the spirit; but failure to depend on this guidance is not due to "moral evil" or wickedness but again is due to ignorance. Second, it must be perceived that the objective experience in pain and poverty is but a reflex of the wrong mental attitude or thought. To be sure, a physical body, to be physical at all, must have the power of sensation and it must be possible for it to have the capacity of unpleasant sensation, since such sensations are to warn us that we are out of harmony with our environment and the law, and that we must get right or perish. But the mind that is stayed on God or is in harmony with the Law will intuitively perceive what is necessary to be done and so will be kept from violating the law of nature. No accident ever befell Jesus because He was in perfect accord with the Father. There are many today who thus "clothe themselves safely round with Infinite Love and Wisdom." "There shall no evil befall *thee*, neither shall any plague come nigh thy dwelling." Thus we perceive that so-called "evil" of mind or body is simply the effect of wrong choices which are due to ignorance; but ignorance is not a moral fault. But the Law is no respecter of persons and if we think limitation and sickness and accident, we shall externalize it. Therefore when we find ourselves surrounded by external limitations which are unpleasant, we must realize that they are but the reflex of our thought.

GOOD AND EVIL BOTH REAL—BUT EFFECTS.

The question now arises as to whether health and wealth are not more *real* than sickness and poverty. Neither is more real than the other. Both are the same primary substance, energy moulded by thought. We can think one into manifestation as easily as the other. We realize that this is quite contrary to the usual concept of the newer teaching. It is said, "Evil, want, sickness, and so on are due to the lack of something. Poverty is a lack of wealth, but lack of something is zero; therefore, there is no poverty. Ignorance is lack of wisdom, but the lack of a thing is zero, therefore there is no ignorance"; and so on, thus claiming that the negative is a lie and therefore the experience is unreal. I am quoting my own former views, for I thought the same thing before I thought clearly enough. It seemed to me that when one thinks health and wealth he gets it; but that when he thinks sickness and poverty he doesn't get it, he only thinks he gets it. This was a mistake. What man sows in thought, that shall he also reap, be it pleasant or unpleasant. All effects are as real as their causes and "the thing exists in the thought as well as the thought in the thing." Again it was a mistake for me to say, for example, that "darkness, being the lack of light, is therefore nothing." The fact remains that the experience of darkness is just as real as that of light. If it were not, I could not be conscious of it. One cannot be conscious of that which is not. If, therefore, I am conscious of poverty or sickness, my consciousness is as true as my consciousness of wealth or health; or else I am conscious of neither. But I am conscious of both. What is needed, therefore, is not that I should change the fact but that I should change the thought that produces the fact.

Again it was wrong for me to say that there can be the absence of something and therefore a nothing. If experience is real enough for me to cognize it and I call it "nothing," I am saying that there is a "nothing" as opposed to the Something which is God or Infinite; and I am therefore positing a dual universe and limiting the Limitless. This is impossible. Therefore my experience of health, wealth, and love, or my experience of poverty, sickness and unhappiness are equally real. But they are **both** effects of my thinking. They are the reflex of my thought. My thought is the cause which takes original substance and moulds it into these forms and experiences. The result is not to be termed either good or evil; neither is the thought. It is not a question of morals but of wisdom. If, therefore, I do not like the effect, I must change the thought. And in order that I may not need to go through all the awful experiences of pain and want in order to learn, I can draw near to the heart of God Who knows all from the beginning; and "the spirit shall teach me all things and guide me into the way of truth."

God Not to Blame for Effects of Wrong Thinking.

The question is always asked, "Where did the first thought of evil come from? and why did God allow evil and suffering in the world? Why does He permit war, famine, and death?" And the answer is: He does not permit it. He has nothing to do with it. He gives us the power to think as individuals. He gives us free will and choice and then leaves it up to us as to what we shall think. If we choose to think in terms of limitation that is our affair, but we must bear the consequences of the Law that we get what we think. We must realize that there is supply enough in the world to satisfy the needs of all. If we fail to take it, it is not the fault or work of God. If we bring pain and loss upon ourselves, it does not involve Him.

We must remember that these effects which we do not like are due to thinking in terms of limitation, and as God never thinks in those terms He cannot cognize their effects. In other words, it is a question if God knows there are wars and death and all the rest of these things. "The Lord is of too pure an eye to behold iniquity." But did not Jesus say, "Not a sparrow falleth to the ground but your Heavenly Father seeth it?" Exactly so, but He does not see it *dying,* He sees it *alive.* God is spirit, He deals with the spirit, and in spirit there is no death. As Jesus quoted "God is not the God of the dead, but of the living. I am the God of Abraham." Unto Him, all are alive.

The Source of Wrong Thought.

It becomes clear therefore that the thought of limitation is to be blamed on no one but ourselves. If we do not like our world and our environment, we must change it by our change of thought. Our environment is of our own making and we can move into the scenes and circumstances that fit our mental outlooks the moment we arrive at the consciousness that will draw us to our desired good. Heaven is a state of consciousness as possible on this plane as any other. Two people on the same street often live in worlds that are as wide apart as the spheres because in the case of one there is constant thought of ill with its physical correspondences, in the other there is the constant thought of good. So we realize that the power to choose what he shall think and how he shall love constitutes the very vital spark of man's individuality. So too he can give or withhold his love from the Supreme Spirit. For God to have endowed him with less than choice would have been to make him a piece of mechanism. But he must pay for the freedom that he enjoys by the suffering that follows *wrong* thinking and failure to love. And his wrong thinking is due to his failure to love or establish harmony between himself and the Infinite Wisdom. For when he withholds his love he is out of harmony with wisdom and cannot be guided by those intuitive processes which keep him from making choices which plunge him into so much pain and unhappiness.

The secret, therefore, of correct living is not found in the study of the negative or so-called "evil" but of the positive or divine life, love and wisdom. If our ideals make us, as we have found in another chapter (Lesson XVI), then *we rise out of limitations by a choice of higher ideals.* In the presence of light, darkness disappears; the rising sun has never looked upon darkness for as it rises darkness flees before it. Love has never looked upon hate; for when love comes, hate disappears. Harmony has never heard discord, for there is none in the presence of perfect wisdom. Wealth can experience no poverty for there is no lack where supply is abundant. Joy knows no sorrow for happiness is complete mistress wherever it comes. Each of these qualities is then the whole truth for us; truth is indivisible, and therefore their presence must be perfect and complete, and nothing else is possible when they are there.

CONCLUSION.

The value of this study therefore is apparent. *The way to cure all so-called ills is the recognition that "God is all in all."* We must not be like the doctor who studies the dead body to find out about life. To study death will not reveal life. We knew a physician who made a profound study of insanity and was so impressed with the thought of it that he lost his reason. It seems well-established that those who specialize in disease usually die of their specialty, a belief in that which is negative. Again it is well known that *materia medica* rarely cures cancer and similar diseases because it deals with the disease; while mental science daily cures large numbers of such cases because it does not see the "case" but only the perfect expression of life. We have known tumors to disappear in a night, cancers and other growths to drop away bodily by the *realization of the positive element, or the presence of life in its wholeness.*

We can come to only one conclusion: the way to cure the ills, and wants, and evils of life, is to forget them and in their place to set the mind on the beautiful, the good and the true. These become your ideal and automatically solve your problem. Whenever you are presented with a problem of lack, in anything, simply select the good or *positive* factor *which before was lacking* and center your mind on that to the exclusion of everything else. Like the baneful dream at night, like the nightmare with its hideous shadows of unreality, all that is false and wrong and ill and tragic flees when we wake from the sleep of ignorance and fear to the truth that God is all in all, and beside Him there is none other. This was the supreme teaching of the Master Metaphysician. The supreme metaphysician is he who knows in his heart that there is only good and only God.

REALIZATION.

I am not dismayed. God is all; and there is none other than He. He guards, He keeps, He holds, He loves. No evil shall befall me, no plague shall come nigh my dwelling. He gives His angels to keep charge over me in all my ways. I am set free in the consciousness of truth. I am at one with the Father in consciousness of life. I see only the good and the true. I will never allow myself to see anything else. God is all. I carry away with me in my heart this song that sings in my soul all day: I admit no thought of ill or want or fear; I admit only truth and love and life. These are God's; and they are mine. God is the only power there is. And all that the Father hath is mine. I accept it and am whole. I give thanks. So be it.

LESSON XIX

THE THING I FEAR.

"THE thing I greatly feared has come upon me." This is a true saying. But why? Because that is exactly the way the Law works. The Universal Creative Intelligence takes the strongest impress of our thought as its model and begins to create each thing after its kind. If fear is our thought then that is our model and it is done unto us as we think. As we saw in the lesson on "Evil," the Law is neutral and impersonal, and having no choice of its own, it acts upon our choice. Our thought and faith are the model on which the Law builds and if we wish a beautiful house we must have beautiful plans. We cannot expect a "mansion in heaven" if our plans call for a dog-house on earth.

We are told by the psychologist that every mental action has a corresponding physical reaction of some sort. Then to hold fear in our thought is to cause it to materialize in the same way. Disease is the thing that appears on the body to correspond to some image of thought held by us either consciously or unconsciously.

Usually we ourselves can trace our trouble back to its mental source, but not always, because it is often an unconscious thing. Frequently we find that the image

113

was produced by a shock of some kind as in the death of or accident to one we love. Or perhaps to some story we have read or heard. Or it may have been due to the race belief or suggestion of fear and disease and belief in it. Or it may be due to our general way of looking at things without any specific or special thought. Or it may be due to some current prevail ing belief in sickness as in an epidemic. One who is sensitive to mental impressions is open to the most subtle suggestion from the many minds about him. In the case of the great influenza epidemic which was due to chaotic world thinking, fear, worry and hatred, we found many minds open to it. Yet, though large numbers died of this fear-thought, we know that those who came under mental treatment were easily and readily cured. There were cases in every degree and progress of the influenza, yet they yielded readily to the treatment. By realizing the perfect peace and calm in the Divine Mind in which we live, move and have our being, and which lives us, moves us, and is the self of us, large numbers of people were cured in one treatment; and even while they were telephoning for relief, they were healed.

Our every word, thought and feeling thus finds expression in our body or personality. Each word or thought is a ruler, though it be king for but an instant; and the law is its servant. Our personality is the aggregate of our thinking expressed in form. The totality of our thinking makes us what we are. The aggregate of the thinking of a normal person is healthy. Therefore, he has health. The chronic invalid is one whose mind consciously or unconsciously dwells more on disease than health.

Some people appear always unlucky. They expect it; and the law works out their misfortune to its bitter conclusion. Others are proverbially "lucky." They expect luck and good fortune therefore smiles upon them. Our attitudes of mind therefore control our destiny. Men who succeed are found to be those who expect success and men who fail are those who most fear failure. Of course in any particular case it is not always possible to trace out the full working of the law of cause and effect, because so many elements work in. Often the habitually fearful have days of hope and the habitually hopeful have days of fear. **What All of Us Need to Do, Therefore, Is to Bring up the Aggregate of Our Thinking for Health, Wealth, and Love So That It Shall Outbalance Any Possible Amount of Negative Thinking.**

We all need to bring our thought up to the highest point of cheer that we possibly can so that we can counteract the currents of fear into which we may for a time allow ourselves to be swept.

And into these currents every one of us tends at times to be drawn through a false idea of sympathy. We allow ourselves to "feel sorry" about ourselves or someone else. The heart of great compassion naturally goes out in loving regard for those who are in the path of error, sorrow, or loss. This is right and natural. But many of us allow this sentiment to degenerate into pity, not for them, but for their misfortune. Instead of doing what we can to alleviate the suffering, we simply condole and "sympathize" with the error, thus allowing ourselves to feel the reality of "evil", or negation and so making ourselves at one with it. **Pity of This Kind Is Evil. Do Not Indulge in It. Do Not Allow Yourself to Be Indulged in It.** How easy it is for us to want others to sympathize with us, to pity us, to feel sorry about us! It is not only a great sign of weakness, it is also very selfish, and it opens us to all their negative thinking about us. "I won't have anybody pity me," said one of the noblest women I ever knew when she was working far beyond her ordinary strength. With an invalid husband, a family, and great responsibilities, she would yet not allow that mental attitude to be held toward her. She rose at length above her difficulties.

Jesus made a remarkable statement at one time. He said, "The Prince of this World cometh and findeth nothing in me." What did He mean? He meant that no thought of lack, or evil, or fear could enter His mind because there was nothing in Him to attract it. The negative thought comes blowing along but it cannot "blow in" on the mind that is positive for there is nothing in that mind to attract or hold it. Hence evil cannot become a reality to that soul. This is the reason why we should place the mind on the highest things because it holds the mind positive only to the best and the worst can "have no part in us" for it does not "find anything in us."

Will this truth help us to get rid of our fears? I do not know. We need to be warned against wrong thinking. We need to know that our fears will destroy us—but then We Want to Forget It. We Must Not Allow Ourselves to Say, "Well, I Expect to Be Destroyed by These Negative Things". Rather we should forget it all by turning our thought to the highest and finest things in which we can find interest "Wherefore dost thou doubt, O ye of little faith?" asks the Great Teacher. "Cheer up," He says constantly. "Be not anxious for your life, what ye shall eat; nor yet for your body, what ye shall put on. For the life is more than the food and the body than the raiment. Consider the ravens, that they sow not, neither reap; which have no store-chamber nor barn; and God feedeth them: of how much more value are ye than the birds! And which of you by being anxious can add one cubit unto the measure of his life. Consider the lilies, how they grow: they toil not, neither do they spin; yet I say unto you, Even Solomon in all his glory was not arrayed like one of these. But if God so clothe the grass which today is and tomorrow is cast into the oven; how much more shall He clothe you, O ye of little faith! . . . Your Father knoweth. . . Fear not, little flock, it is your Father's pleasure to give you the kingdom."

It is faith and love that solves our problems.

It is love. Love walks on the waves to still the turbulent sea of life. Love quiets the storm and brings the frail vessel to a safe harbor. Love says,

"It is I, be not afraid." It is love that says, "Lo, I am with you alway, even unto the ends of the earth."

> It is love that lifts the burden,
>   Love that lightens every task;
> Fear not thou, but cease thy struggle,
>   Love will give you all you ask.
> Love is God, and all about you
>   Breathes His presence on the air,
> Unseen hands are raised to help you
>   By the Presence everywhere.
>
> Love is life; its rising surges
>   Sweep in tides around the wreck,
> Lift and bear it to the ocean
>   With the captain on the deck.
> Thou the captain; God, the ocean,
>   Love the power that moves the tide:
> Pilot past the bar and breakers,
>   Love is acting as thy guide.

REALIZATION.

God is in His heaven and all is right with the world. I will fear no evil for Thou art with me. No evil shall befall me and no plague come nigh my dwelling. He has given His angels charge over me to keep me in all my ways. They shall bear me up in their hands lest I dash my foot against a stone. I am kept by that perfect love that casts out all fear. Fear cannot come near me because my mind is stayed on the highest and best. (Then argue it all out with yourself. How can I escape from this thing? Surely it cannot be by fearing it.) I look you mentally in the face and defy you, discouragement and fear. You have no part in me for I am above you. I will not pity myself because that only makes my fear more real. (Suppose it is some feeling that you have a dreadful disease upon you. To fear it will only make it worse. There is no disease known that will not yield to truth and faith of those who are determined to be well, and the way to get well is to stop fearing and go to thinking healthful and hopeful thoughts.) I know that all power is given unto me in heaven and on earth. I will use this God-power in me and I am thankful for it. Thoughts of self-pity and fear have no influence with me. I will not allow any one to pity me for that will only fasten this thing upon me. The Prince of this world, fear and sickness, comes to me but they do not find a welcome here. There is nothing in me to give them a welcome. Yes, perfect love casts out all fear from *me*. (If it is fear of business failure, treat it in the same way. To fear it is to bring it on you. You cannot do one bit of good by worrying. That will only reduce your strength in an emergency.) He that clothes the lily will look after my interests. I am safe in the assurance that if this particular thing should fail, there is something better to come for me. (We have known of many cases where present failure was simply the prelude to a greater success. Sometimes the accumulated thoughts of failure and sorrow or in-

harmony have been swept away by flood or fire or
bankruptcy only to sweep the mind clean for higher
attainment.   Thousands have thus begun at the bot-
tom only to climb still higher in the new work.   To
fear failure will not help.   Have faith. ⸱This is the
one great essential.   Have faith in yourself.   Have
faith in others.   Have faith in the future.   Have faith
in God.   Courage and faith are half the battle.   Determination, will, and work are the other half.   You
can if you think you can.)   I know I can succeed and
I will succeed.   I am success.   I am courage.   I am
faith.   I am the victory.   Faith is the victory that
overcomes the world, and I have all the faith there is.
(Then concentrate your thought for a moment on the
positive thing you want.   Make up your mind that
you will have the best and the best only.   If you do
not know now just what course to follow, there is a
Mind in you that does.   Depend on it.   Resolve to be
lead by the Divine Wisdom that speaks through you.
Step out in faith on the new venture for health, wealth,
or love and expect great things.   The spirit in you
will soon lead you into the best.)   Now let this good
come to me.   Let it come in the best possible way.
Let me be lead by Divine Wisdom.   Let me be prospered.   Thou givest me above all I ask or think, and
I am satisfied that all is well with me.   I render thanks.
(Spend a moment on the Divine Wisdom within you,
and go your way with a song in your heart. **Let It
Be Done Unto Thee Even as Thou Wilt.)**   So be it!

LESSON XX.

NOTHING MATTERS.

SO many of the ills of the world are due to hurt feelings and worry over what other people say and do that we need a new motto. Let us try this, "Nothing matters." Jesus exclaims, "What is that to thee? Follow thou me." That has nothing to do with you unless you allow it. Why do you allow yourself to worry and fuss if someone seems preferred before you? There is enough for you to do. You have your place somewhere. What does it matter to you if your neighbor does act unneighborly? He won't have the opportunity to hurt you unless you care. Why should you go about with an aching heart because people won't take your advice, or insist on doing things in a different way from that which you approve? Will that change them any? Suppose that some member of your family is a bit uncouth or even rude, don't you see that you are only aggravating it by "caring?" When you show your indifference, not defiantly, but by really not "allowing it to matter," you will see the things change. You say, business is going wrong and I must worry! Worry will only hasten the end. You need to save yourself so that you will have a clear mind to act in case of emergency or a change for the better. Say, "nothing matters."

Sensitive-minded people are always undergoing some new form of mental torture. And the thing for which they suffer doesn't matter much after all. And they wouldn't suffer at all, if they would refuse to be annoyed. And if you really do care very much, you cannot remedy things by "caring" You are really being negative and just suffering. You can never get the most out of life by depending on anybody or anything for your happiness. You must be free of dependence on all: Otherwise you will be subject to chance and change. You will become a victim of circumstance. You will truly enjoy friends and things only as you know how to live without them. Shall you make a necessity of your friend? Then you make him your servant. Rather will you say, "I will extract the full joy of this hour. Today is all there is. If tomorrow he goes away or seeks companionship elsewhere, then we have already extracted all there is of value between us. To companion with him now would be to fan coals to a glow to make me think there is a fire. It does not matter; I must go on to new experiences."

So, too, you must know how to live without *things* or you are become their slave. Rather should you extract from all the essence of joy for the hour and as the bee sips the nectar and passes on, so you pass from good to good because no *one* thing has become a necessity to you. Take everything but cling to nothing; then indeed do things become your servant, not you their slave.

To fear loss, to feel hurt, to mourn over that which is passing is to give reality to the negative side of life, and to draw greater evil in its train. By the law of attraction we draw outer things to correspond to our inner thought and feeling, and soon the thing we greatly feared has come upon us. Rather let us say, "What is that to me? I really don't care. Now I start forgetting." Then we are ready for positive thinking. Then we put up to the Creative Mind the image of the good we desire and the law of correspondences will bring it to us. We claim from the law anything we desire from friends to fortune, but we do not demand this particular friend or that identical fortune. That is hypnotism and dictation to the law as to *how* it shall work. That might be to demand something that will bring us hurt. Rather must we hold up the *perfect idea* of the good we seek and let Divine Mind specialize it for us and manifest it in form.

We must follow the command, "Follow thou me." We are to follow not after the negative, but after the positive; we are to seek first the kingdom of con- sciousness, the inner *spirit* and faith in life, and all *things* shall be added unto us.

"Let's start forgetting!
There are so many things to lay away
In graves—dead hates and fears, and doubts
that flay,
And all these little faults scarce worth a
groan.

There are so many black days we have
             known!
There is no use regretting!
                Let's try forgetting.

  Let's start forgetting!
A thought of envy is no pleasant guest,
And hatred nourished leaves no peace or rest;
A tear's no thing to treasure; and no strife
Becomes a corner stone to fuller life.
  Away with grief and fretting!
                Let's start forgetting."

REALIZATION.

I am now entered into the secret place of the Most
High. I am resting in the presence of Spirit. The
world is shut out. I am shut in the temple of my soul.
I am in touch with all that is. I am drawing from the
springs of life and peace and plenty. I am waiting
on the Lord that He may renew my strength. My mind
is open, my soul is receptive, my body receives the
healing touch. In this vast quiet of spirit I am un-
afraid and undisturbed. No evil can befall me here.
Nothing negative matters, for it has no real power
and I am not afraid of it. I see only the good, I hear
only the good. Now everything seems good and
beautiful to me. I trust in the restoring and creative
power of spirit. I have faith in God and I am satisfied. I give thanks.

LESSON XXI.

COURAGE REGAINED.

LIFE is not in the body but in the spirit. Its length is not to be measured by the physical or animal strength but by the spirit within. People who have lived to "a ripe old age" have by no means been just those who started out with a robust physique. The athlete is a type of manhood, but not the highest type. Manhood consists in other things than the body. The chief concern of metaphysics is not to get the body well but to get the mind to realize its wellness, and to realize the inner sources of life. When this is accomplished fully, the body will take care of itself. So why should you be discouraged because you do not have all the physical vigor you desire at the present time? It will come to you of itself when you get your mind right. And physical vigor is not necessarily in the size of the muscles. It is a well-known fact that the will of man prolongs the life beyond the usual measure. Even if you have long periods of "the ups and downs" of physical well-being before you realize perfect health, that should not discourage you. You will live just as long and the experiences through which you are now passing may bring you into a clearer recognition of some of the truths you want to know.

And no one should be discouraged because he has failed to make steady and consistent progress in any-thing, whether physically, mentally, or spiritually. The path of human life usually lies in the canyons as well as upon the mountain peak and there are valleys of vision as well as mountains of vision as the Bible shows us. The man in the valley can see the stars even as the man on the mountain. This does not mean that we should be content with the narrower views of the valley; but it does show that even at the beginning of the course we have inspiration to endeavor for we have a star of vision from the very first step.

History and science concur in showing that progress, mental, physical and spiritual, comes through a process much like the rising of a tide. The waves roll in on the beach and recede, roll and recede; and the tide gains on the land almost imperceptibly. Yet each succeeding ambitious wave hurls itself forward a little farther than any that has gone before, and as hour follows hour the high point in the tide is finally reached. A study of botany reveals this process in the growth of plants. We are told that the plant shoots upwards for a way, then crouches down or draws back as though to conserve its strength. Afterward it repeats the process—and so it grows. Or take another illustration. On the battlefields the soldiers sometimes burst through the line and make great progress. Their ambition is to make a quick dash on the open fields and defeat the enemy; but this cannot be done. They must delay, one day, two days, a week. They must conserve the results already gained; they must get ready for another successful advance. So this is in mental science. You cannot live every day at the same pitch of intensity. You appear to fall back. Really, if you have the scientific attitude, you are conserving results for another advance.

Now you are not to suppose that you yourself will always be conscious of this process going on within. A seed planted in the subjective mind goes on growing of itself. If you have planted there a true seed of confidence in the healing power of mind, if the seed is confidence specifically that the ailment from which you now seem to suffer is being eliminated, then the process goes on without the conscious attention of your mind. There may even be moments of depression in which you think your faith in the matter is gone, but if beneath it all there is that steady *tendency* of the thought toward health and happiness, then in that case the process is still going on within you. That is one reason for having a healer. *He knows* even when you do not that this is the unfailing process. Though for the moment your conscious mind is rebellious and you feel pain or unhappiness, *he* does not recognize this. He sees you only as you potentially are—*well and whole.* He plants the seed of health in the great within of your mind and soul. It will grow there unless you are too rebellious so that you entirely uproot the seed. You *must* be awakened to the necessity of more *trust.* You are not to blame for the condition you are in but for the *cause.* You must have more faith. Fear and worry and nervous tension are effects, not causes. You are to blame not for the effects but for the causes. Trust—that is the only way. Say to yourself if you must, "I don't know just how that thing works; I do know I have had light enough to show that this is my only way out. I will therefore follow it. I will therefore *believe* in the process even though I cannot yet see the results, nor feel the working of the law." Columbus started on faith to a new world. You are starting to a new world. If I am not mistaken, you have just about reached the point where the crew wants to put you in chains and take you home again although you are only a few miles off the shore of the new country. Don't Let These Little Doubt Devils Get the Best of You. Insist on Reaching the New Land.

Did you ever watch the light from a light-house on a dangerous coast? It does not shine with a steady glare. The light pierces the gloom for a moment and then disappears. Experience has shown that this is the most successful kind of a light. Faith is that kind of a light-house. Understanding is that kind of a light-house. It comes in flashes. One flash has come to you and then another. Or you may liken the light to flashes that have come to you from light-house minds. They illumine your way for a moment, then recede to enable you to move forward under your own and not a borrowed light. Presently you will recognize the landmarks and make your way into the harbor. So if the way may at times seem dark and fearful, remember the principle of the light-house, sight it, and sail on.

You have nothing to fear. Your case is not an unusual one. You have not launched out far enough into the deep. "Let the shore line go." Sail for the harbor of your soul and of health.

The true soul never accepts defeat.

Defeated? Never! Held back, confined, perhaps;
But only as the current of a stream:
The rushing torrent of my life still gathers
And swirling, threatens the obstructing beam.

Discouraged? I deny the imputation;
The silent forces of my life flow on;
The deep resistance of the soul grows stronger
And all my fears of foe and fate are gone.

Because I know some day the channel opens
And my determined will has right of way—
I wait, but *gather force each hour of waiting*
And scorn the coward's whisper of dismay.

Above the dam the waters lie but deeper,
The swirling eddies token more of life:
Who measures strength with fate has stronger
    muscle,
Emerges more a man from every strife.

Valiantly strive, nor heed opposing forces:
No force avails thy genius to control:
God sends His rain to feed thy flood, which rising
Sweeps all before the onrush of thy soul.

The Law of Mind in Action.

REALIZATION.

Three times a day at regular intervals seek three or four minutes of quiet and perfect relaxation and repeat to yourself the following: "With God all things are possible. I will fear no evil for Thou art with me. I have faith in God. **All** things work together for good to them that love God. I am discovering the new country." Say it firmly, confidently. This will put you in the right state for the working of the deeper law.

LESSON XXII.

CREATIVE IMAGINATION.

THE mind of man is naturally imaginative; the normal man sees things in visions, dreams dreams —all normal men do.

It is not confined to the unbalanced brain. Says Shakespeare in "A Midsummer Night's Dream"

> "The lunatic, the lover, and the poet,
> Are of imagination all compact."

And one reason why more attention has not been given to this creative faculty has been this very fact that imagination appears in dreams, fantasy, intoxication and insanity, as well as in philosophy, poetry, and inventive genius. We have turned off Shakespeare's significant words with the remark that of course every lover is a lunatic imagining that he can write poetry, and to say that "the lunatic, the lover and the poet are of imagination all compact," is a poetic way of saying one and the same thing, that imagination is the mental equivalent of lunacy. However, there are too many evidences of the power of creative thought in imagination for us to disregard it, and we shall find that imagination has more than gauzy wings. Gregory, the author of a text-book on psychology, says, "In creative imagination the leading process is construc-

131

tion according to three laws—of the true, the beautiful and of the good. These are the very highest acts of which human genius is capable." Another writer states that "if it were not for imagination, improvements in the arts and sciences and therefore in the general conditions of peoples, would be wholly due to accident."

What Is Imagination?

What then is this great faculty which affects the destiny of peoples, forms the basis of a faith, and makes the course of true love run rough or smooth? It is the act or power of the mind which sweeps all the experiences of the past and present, all our thoughts and observations into the lap of memory, and then, like a child with its blocks, takes them up one by one and builds a structure like the model of the past, that is, reproduces the past, or fashions them into *new forms and combinations entirely different from the old.* In the one case it assists the memory, in the other it creates and is the incubation of art, invention, science, and discovery.

The Use of the Imagination.

That we should exercise the visualizing power of the imagination is commended by the great Teacher, Who said, "Whatsoever things ye desire when ye pray, believe that ye have received them; and ye shall receive them." This is transcendent imagination. It requires not only that we see clearly and completely, but so clearly and completely that it is as though we had already objectively realized it. You are urged to form a complete picture of the thing you desire, to see it in its wholeness, as a perfect thing, just as it will be when received. This is the fundamental psychology of it; you cannot receive what you do not understand; you must have an ideal of what you desire. And the formulation of this model or ideal is the work of the imagination. And it is only when a man knows what it is that he wants that he can hope to attain it.

It is in this formative power of the imagination, which creates an ideal toward which a man may strive, that we find the basis of modern metaphysical movements, both in the matter of health and prosperity. However intelligent its followers may be as to the fundamental nature of the process, this is the essential secret of the activity and success of the movement.

For it would be most true in regard to health. First, there is the image of a perfect body, the image of the perfect organ, which is the creation of the imagination. Then each drop of blood that distils from the heart bears the imprint of that idea, carries its precious freight to the affected organ, paints it with the perfection of its own pigment. At the same time nerve and neuron carry the imperious mandate of the brain that all must be well there. Thought centers upon it and all the vital forces acting in obedience to the will tend to restore the broken tissue. This helps us to understand why we must lay stress on the idea of perfection. Man, the perfect idea, is ideally a perfect organism.

This is good psychology, for the finer the model the more perfect the production. If we can "image" perfection in spite of the immediate claim of the senses, we have the most satisfactory model after which to pattern the body and mind and estate.

The Importance in Thinking.

It is quite clear from this, I believe, that it is of inestimable importance that whatever enters the mind should be of highest quality and character, since it is to furnish the material out of which the models of things are to be made.

Imagination is destructive as well as constructive. It can unmake us as well as make. If we hang upon the walls of memory pictures of passion, hate, lust, greed, murder, suicide, robbery, demon faces of sin— peeping out from very sheet of the modern newspaper —with thoughts of failure, poverty, sickness and death, we shall at length use these pigments to paint the life of our own future. Or if we mix good and evil imagery, we shall chisel a character as dreadful as the centaur with a man's head and torso and the body of a horse, or the fabled monster with the head of a human, the body of a lion, and the wings and claws of an eagle, or of the grotesque gargoyle on the roof of the temple which represents the demon shut out from the sacred precincts.

Our Future in Our Own Control.

Nothing seems to me clearer than that man has it very much in his control as to what shall be his future

through the proper exercise of his imagination. Nat
ure has endowed us with rich powers; it is a pity that
we have linked them up with insanity or turned them
all aside as some form of fanaticism, the unique possession of some religious faith. And it is a pity that
we have been rearing our children on this basis. Imagination is the chief characteristic of childhood.

> "Trailing clouds of glory
> Do we come from God, Who is our home:
> Heaven lies about us in our infancy."

The child lives much of the time in a world far
removed from the evidence of our senses; his block
of wood is a speeding engine with flying wheels, the
trough in which he sails his boat is the boundless blue
of the sea, and he freights the argosy of his hope with
treasures from the storehouse of his mind, and shifts
the sails and flies before the driving winds to the harbor of his heart's desire. His inanimate objects have
life, they laugh and sing, they weep and walk and
fight, for all the world like the mythical heroes of
Greece and Rome. Every child has creative instinct.

CULTIVATE IMAGINATION IN THE CHILD.

Nature provides faculties of imagination. The fault
with us is that we begin to beat it out of the children
at an early age. Not literally, but figuratively, although
evidence is not lacking that we use more than moral
suasion to this end. But imagination merits a better

fate, it should be turnèd to account in the creation of character and a greater destiny

There is a power sufficient in childhood to produce character and destiny beyond anything that the world has ever witnessed, if it could be successfully drawn out. Nature provides the mould for the raw material in imagination. It only remains to discipline this imagination, put it under the control of the will, teach the child how to test its products by judgment, not only to make it the strongest educational factor in our schools, but also the impulsive power to a lofty destiny for the individual and the race.

The Danger.

I think I have said enough to show that imagination, if put into proper operation, will be of supreme worth in the creation of health, success, character and destiny. It is no strange esoteric power. And it is by using this force in strong conjunction with those other admirable forces with which man has been endowed by Providence that we can create for ourselves an ever-widening world. Our destiny is in our own hands; following the law we may rise from height to height Says Henri Bergson, the prophet of idealism, "In a conscious being, to exist is to change, to change is to mature, to mature is to go on creating ourselves endlessly." Wisely may we use our powers for an ever enlarging existence.

REALIZATION.

"He that believeth on me, the works that I do shall he do also."

I know that this refers to my own spiritual nature. I do believe on the Indwelling Christ. I do believe in the "Christ within me, the hope of glory." I do believe on the high nature of spirit in me. I am confident that I have the spirit of life, love, and freedom in me. I am confident that the Master taught truly Who said, "Greater works than these shall ye do," and "All power is given unto me in heaven and on earth." Therefore I do now believe in the works that shall follow my word of faith and today I utter that word in perfeet serenity of spirit. "Let it be done unto me, even as I will." It is so done and I am glad and thankful. I am led. I am prospered. I am blessed. I am inspiration to all men, because I am faithful to God and His promises. I shall give thanks for the gift of life and faith. So be it.

ONE-POINTEDNESS.

NO principle of metaphysics is more essential than one-pointedness. We must have a real idea or image and we must adhere to it. The Bible clearly expresses this principle. We read, "One thing have I desired of the Lord, that will I seek after." Or, "This one thing I do: I press on toward the mark of the high calling." Or, again, "He that wavereth is like a wave of the sea, driven by the wind and tossed. Let not that man think he shall receive anything of the Lord."

We see here that there is a two-fold demand: first, that we definitely decide upon the thing we desire; second, that we refuse to keep changing the desire. The reason for this is clear to the metaphysician. He knows that he will obtain from the Great Creative Mind only what he impresses upon that Mind. For example, let us suppose a worker in iron to be casting the engine for an automobile. To do so, he must fashion his sand-mould in the shape desired and then run in the molten iron. The shape desired must be that of an engine, and nothing else. If the moulder is careless of the shape of the mould, the moulten iron will take an indefinite shape.

On the same principle, the demonstrator must realize that his thought is the mould or pattern which the Creative Mind must follow. He must fashion his thought definitely; and into the mould the creative force will flow on the principle that the flow of substance and energy is always *in vacuo,* which in this case is the attitude of *definite* expectancy. And we receive from the Spirit only what we look to receive. The Spirit is ready to pour Itself out in fullest measure, but can never fill a different room than the one made ready for it. Christ illustrates this when He says, "Behold, I stand at the door and knock. If any man will open it, I will come in and sup with him and he with me." *We* must open the door.

The Creative Spirit enters only the door that is open and the room that is made ready. So then we must have a definite, positive, perfect idea of what we desire. Having it, we should cling to it and never waver either in the image of what we want or in our expectancy of receiving it.

The moment you project a desire or create an image and say, "Now let this thing *be,* let it externalize in fact," you have begun the creative process. The Spirit then takes up that image and begins to work upon it. If we let it alone, and wait faithfully, that is, in faith, it will at length materialize. The image or prototype has become a reality in the realm of mind or spirit. It is the seed involving the plant and the flower which by the law of growth will ultimately mature. We may speak of that prototype as in the *present* tense; as we say, "I have perfect digestion." Now, at the moment

we may be *manifesting* an imperfect digestion, but we
are "judging not by appearances but rather right
judgments." So we say, "I *have* perfect digestion."
If we do this with faith we create the perfect mould
or image or prototype. This the *present* tense. The
Spirit begins to work upon our model and ultimately
brings out the perfected or externalized object of our
desire. This is the *future* tense, using relative terms.
Now we can say, "I have perfect digestion," alluding
not only to the image in the Creative Mind but also
to the now realized external fact. This is the process
of demonstration and this is what Jesus meant when
he said, "When ye pray, believe ye have received it
(know that it exists now, potentially) and ye shall
have it" (since it will ultimately materialize).*

In the second place, we must beware, lest, between
the formation of the image and its logical and ultimate
realization, we change the character of our desire or
ruin our model by lack of faith. We must therefore
be consistent in our expectations. We must await the
result without fear or change, for "he that wavereth
is like a wave of the sea driven by the wind and
tossed. Let not that man think he shall receive anything from the Lord or Spirit."

REALIZATION.

I will not recognize any imperfection in life today.
I know that alone is real to which I gave consciousness;

*The student is asked to read Chapter XXIX, Part II, in this connec-
tion to see how Spirit takes the *idea and gives it form,* when *we* do
not know how to visualize or image it for ourselves. Yet even in
this, *definiteness of idea* is required of us.

and I will not endow evil and lack with a power they
do not possess. I will not see evil; I will not hear
evil; I will not speak evil. No one can talk to me of
wrong and imperfection, for I will not listen. I will
not be receptive to negative thoughts or suggestions.
None of these things move me, for I am above them.
I am above all pettiness and smallness. I am receptive
only to positive thoughts and acts. Today I am positive minded. I am resolute, courageous and full of
faith in God, in men, and in myself. What I do, I
do with vigor; what I say, I say with decision. I am
strong, forceful, calm, poised; I rest in the quiet confi
dence of one who knows that back of him is unlimited life, love, and wisdom. "All power is given unto
me in heaven and on earth."

LESSON XXIV.

FAITH, AN ATTITUDE OF MIND.

WHEN we come to study faith in the light of the new truth we find ourselves reaching quite a different conclusion regarding it than perhaps we once did. We no longer conceive of faith as a desperate hold upon a mysterious and uncertain future. We find that faith in its true sense is an attitude of mind. It is confident expectancy. It is a quality of mind designed for immediate use in the practical affairs of life. It is not creed or religion; it is steady confidence. Faith connects the immediate present with the immediate future. It is certain knowledge that has not reached the point of demonstration as yet where it can be subjected to the ordinary tests of logic and experience, but is just as certain of itself as though it could. It is the positive conviction not only that the real is derived from the good, and the good from the real, but also that the best will happen to me and mine both now and in the days to come.

> "And I will trust that He who heeds
>   The life that hides in mead and wold,
> Who hangs the alder's crimson beads
>   And paints the mosses green and gold
> Will still, as He has done, incline
>   His gracious care to me and mine."

Faith is, therefore, also a conviction of God's present and continuous care. It is a winged spirit fluttering out a little way into the dark while we follow. As we follow, all grows light. Faith is the star that glimmers in what would otherwise be darkness, what just beyond the present is darkness to all but the man who has faith and knows.

Yet faith is not some peculiar and indefinable mystery designed to reveal glorious and dim futures, but is an attribute of mind as real as reason. It is a higher perceptive power of the mind, a finer sense that enables us to perceive things possible. Faith is not a stationary thing; we should not speak of the faith, because faith always keeps ahead of us. Faith of yesterday is experience today and history tomorrow. By faith, inventions are made; by faith, a Panama canal is dug; by faith, science discovers the stars. Most of the great discoveries of science have followed the venture of faith. Science does not work in the dark; it works in the *light* of faith. Faith is thus an attribute of the mind designed for present practical use. It becomes a business asset to the commercial man; we call the man who has it far-sighted. It is the guiding star to the explorer. It is the power to know before a thing comes that it will come or can come. We expect faith to be of Practical use in a practical, work-a-day world because we know that the Kingdom of Heaven is now and that it is our privilege to get the Benefits of the Kingdom Now, not merely hope for them later.

Does this include faith as belief in God? Certainly. Belief in Christ? By all means. But not a mystic and indefinable feeling or emotion. A belief in God **Now**, active **Now**, present **Now**, co-operating **Now**, discerned **Now**; a belief in Christ as present in every soul, beautiful, serene, pure, inspired by love, and active now.

Says Lyman Abbot: "The spirit that was in Christ is the Holy Spirit. To seek it, to possess it, to live in harmony with it and under its guidance and direction, is to be a Christian. This is what Paul means when he says he desires above all things to be found in Christ, 'not having mine own righteousness, which is of the law'—that is, the kind of righteousness which comes from obedience to rules and regulations—'but that which is through the faith **of** Christ, the righteousness which is **of** God **by** faith'; that is, the kind of righteousness which flows spontaneously and naturally from an inward life of fellowship with God. Please to do right, then do as you please—that is Christian living."

Have faith if you will in

"That last, far-off, divine event
Toward which the whole creation moves,"

but have faith greater, more wonderful—a belief in Emmanuel, that is, **God with Us Now**, loving us, lifting us, lighting our way. To have such a faith is to live

in constant touch with God. It is not only to believe
in the power of God, but also to believe He is using
that power **Now** in our behalf. Thus we see that
faith is the faculty of the mind that sees the further
possibilities in us and in the world, that encourages
us to explore and develop the new fields of consciousness. Every time we yield to the urge of faith, we find
ourselves entering new fields of experience, discovering
new possibilities of enjoyment and service in religion,
morals, business, social life, national life. Life is an
illimitable sea. Faith is the telescope which we hold
in our hand as our vessel ploughs her way along. By
it we can see ahead in the course, the dangers to be
avoided, the storms that threaten, the harbors and the
islands that invite.

Man's Divine Nature Assures Him of the Illimitable Capacities of Faith.

You are not vile dust which by magic of God can be
spiritualized and drawn up to Him in some distant,
uncertain place; you are a spirit, soul, in possibility as
pure as God; and faith is the power that awakens your
divine nature, shows you your spiritual endowments,
urges you to test and explore the infinite realm of your
inner consciousness and bring out into practical life
and action the things you find there. Faith is the power
that enables you to sell all that you have—fear, dis-
trust, worry, shame, ignorance, and to purchase the
pearl of great price—the consciousness of the limitless
power of your own soul; for within you are all the

potentialities and possibilities of the Kingdom of Heaven.

God is in **You**, the personal God, at all times; but some do not recognize Him, or claim His guidance and help. Such people do not have the vision of the spiritually enlightened; they do not have the unlimited vision; they have the foresight of reason, but not the heightened perspective of faith. Faith connects the soul that does not recognize God, with the God within and without, and reveals and releases the power that operates through Him.

Faith Gets Results only if Persisted in.

Persistence in faith is essential to success. There is thus nothing that cannot be accomplished through faith. We may secure anything we wish in intellect, in property, in health, in spirituality, through it. But the great difficulty comes in the fact that few people hold to their faith long enough to accomplish anything. They are always in a state of fluctuation. Today having faith in one thing, tomorrow in another; today having faith in faith, and tomorrow having faith in nothing. James says of such a one· "He that wavereth is like a wave of the sea, driven with the wind and tossed, let not that man think he shall receive anything of the Lord." Such people walk by faith for a while, then they see something they very much desire to do which does not fit well with their faith, so they leave the path of faith for a time; they do the inconsistent thing, such as to say the cutting word, perform the unkind act, get the

best of another in a bargain, tell a falsehood to gain
a desired point.

After this they return to the path of faith, but it
is not so satisfactory and they have lost ground, because if we wish to get anywhere we must **Keep at
It.** When we leave the path of faith, we have difficulty
in finding it again. Let him who would test the truth
of the Bible, **"All Things** work together for good to
them that love God", put his whole faith in faith and
believe positively that **All Things** are his. If he persists unceasingly, verily he shall have his reward.

The world calls today for men of faith. The Kingdom of Heaven opens only to this key, and many men
and women are kept from their highest usefulness
because they are afraid or ashamed to use the key and
enter the kingdom. They fear loss of friends, respect
of friends, or that they will lose the sweetness of old
associations. They do not realize that if they enter
the Kingdom of Heaven they will find more than com-
pensation for anything they may lose. And there can
be no real loss to the man of faith.

FEAR KEEPS OUT FAITH.

Fear keeps many beautiful souls hanging in indecision between the old interpretation of faith and the
new. The old faith said, "God's ways are past finding"; the new accepts the promise that "with God all
things are possible" and goes forth to make claim
upon it. In Jesus' parable the laborers got their pay
every day. So we are to begin at once to enjoy the

pleasures and treasures of the Kingdom. If we are
not enjoying them something is wrong somewhere.
We have either misapplied our faith or else been spas-
modic in our application of it. No faculty has been
given to man that is not meant to be applied **Now**.
Faith is so meant. We ought to have abundance of
the things we need—nor think poverty in estate, mind,
or friendship a sign of spirituality. We shall find it
a sign of spirituality **to Have All Things**.

Sometimes, even to those who have true and persistent faith, there will come times when everything
looks dark. Apparently faith has failed us. But if
we persist in faith we shall soon find the darkness
brushed aside and a brighter light than we have ever
known before will shine forth to guide our pathway.
There can be no real darkness or failure to the man
or woman of faith. Apparent failure will for such a
man or woman turn out to be a door to better things;
the seeming defeat of the good today will be the recognized victory tomorrow. *Only have faith in faith,*
and your faith will save you, and you shall "Go in
peace." Faith will turn any course, light any path,
save any situation, relieve any distress, bring joy out
of sorrow, peace out of strife, friendship out of enmity,
Heaven out of hell. Faith can do anything. Faith is
God at **work**.

REALIZATION.

I now rest in the care-free peace of faith. I **do not**
fear, because infinite love and faith abide in me, I

rest, rest, rest! How sweet the word to me. I rest! I rest physically; I rest mentally; I rest in my spirit in the deep calm of eternal peace, for I am one with the Father. "There remaineth therefore a rest for the people of God." I feel an infinite expansion in consciousness: I am slipping out into the infinite life where I may contact God and good at every point. I am not less myself, but more my true self, for I am one with the Infinite Life and Wisdom. I shall return from my quiet hour to life's work and problems with the infinite light of wisdom to guide me and of faith to inspire me. I give thanks,

LESSON XXV.

MENTAL POISE.

DURING the influenza epidemic a friend of mine suddenly found herself caught in the tornado of chaotic thinking and the symptoms made their appearance. She told us about it the next day.

"Yesterday my head and back ached, my throat was sore and I could not keep my feet warm," and seeing our expression of concern she added, "Otherwise I was all right."

"What was all right?" I asked, laughing.

"My mind," she answered calmly.

One who knew the truth less and lived more to the law of fear might have felt alarmed, but not she. She recognized that she had left an opening in her mind for the entrance of the disease-thought and she calmly went to work to cast it out again, and to realize the presence of all-perfect life. "Thou wilt keep him in perfect peace, whose mind is stayed on Thee," says the Psalmist.

One should never be frightened in the presence of negative thoughts and conditions. Simply recognize that they have only as much power as your thought gives to them, as darkness exists only so long as the light remains away from it. Your positive thought is the light and fear and disease are the darkness. You

150

have only to bring in a good thought and the darkness will disappear.

"Ye shall know the truth and the truth shall make you free," said the Divine Revealer. "What is truth?" asks the world in the words of Pilate. And the reply of the Christ is that "for this cause came I into the world," that men might know the truth. "I am the truth." Yet it is not the personal Christ alone Who is to be known, but the **Mind** of Christ. "Have this mind in you which was also in Christ Jesus, our Lord," said Paul. That is to say, we must come to that knowledge of self and God and the universe which Christ had. We must have His mind and understanding before we can come to His character and "be therefore perfect, even as our Father in heaven is perfect."

To acquire this "mind", we must learn to discern all things spiritually, we must perceive the real behind the seeming, and we must deny all that is contrary to a perfect spiritual creation. We must know that man innately is perfect; the true self is divine, for so only would it be possible to attain the outer perfection which Jesus demands. Knowing this truth, we shall be made free from all the ills of human thought and experience.

This is a deep truth but not a mystery. The enlightened soul knows this to be an elementary truth of metaphysics. The awakening soul must constantly and consciously seek and demand of himself the true and the real. When pain or adversity or melancholy or fear appear to manifest themselves, he must say,

"This is not mine. I will not accept it. I will know only the good and the true."

Sometimes this will appear very hard, but if we constantly repress wrong thinking and encourage good, which is the result of right thinking, we shall gradually grow into the sure knowledge of that truth which is to make us free.

We all have asked, "What is truth?" and some of us have found the answer by growing into that attitude of mind and heart which sees and accepts only the good and the true which exists for us all. We all must **"Grow in the truth."** Happy is that man or woman who with hopeful heart persists in "spite of weakness, lameness, blindness" of the human spirit to grow into the divine mind, for then he "shall know the **Truth**, and the truth shall **Make Him Free**."

REALIZATION.

When you feel yourself caught in the grasp of the negative thought, calmly seek the "place of repose." This is in the quiet contemplation of spirit and spiritual reality. I am spirit. I am life. I am in the Divine Mind. Nothing exists but God. No evil can fall upon spirit and the spiritual mind. My mind is right. My heart rests in the peace of this confidence. "Thou wilt keep him in perfect peace whose mind is stayed on Thee."

Why do you sing today? Still hides his face, the sun,
And all is sad the same as when your grief begun.
You do not know the joy that sings in me today,

Because it all is gone; I've cast it all away.
What is it you cast off; can grief and pain be cast,
Can all your loss and woe be buried in the past?
But still confess you see, the strain and stress is gone,
Some weight has rolled away; mine eyes not woe-
begone.
The pain has left my head; that strain here in my side
Has vanished in the sea, as shores cleansed by the tide.
The tide? What tide? I see, some change come over
you,
An atmosphere, a calm, a radiance, 'tis true.
Whence does it spring? Ah, friend reveal this thing
to me,
That I may find your joy, that I your secret see.
It came at dawn, this peace; there lighted in my soul
A wondrous light, that cleansed my mind and made me
whole.
It "cleansed your mind?" "You mock my deep desire
to know.
"Your mind was cleansed," my friend?
Dost change the body so?
'Tis so indeed, 'tis so! Trust took the place of fear;
Love took the place of loss; and joy, of sorrow drear.
Pain vanished with the thought of ever-present love,
I caught a view of God—within—not up above.
In me! In me; within! His kingdom is within!
Where God is, pain is not, where love is, gone is sin.
I breathe a newer life; I live in Spirit now;
And not to fear or pain, but just to Truth I bow.

*My heart was changed at once, my mind changed with
      my heart;*
*Love showed the way   its heal-
      ing part.*

LESSON XXVI.

THE WILL TO WIN AND PROSPERITY.

"THEY can because they think they can," says
Virgil of the winners in the boat race. The
will to win is the first need of the day. Resolve to go
out today with the victor's mind. "Well begun is half
done," is a true saying. You hold the day in the
hollow of your hand this morning. Wisely have great
men exalted the human will, for one must greatly
desire a thing before he can hope to have it. Nor is it
really worth having unless we want it enough to make
some resolutions about it. I will win today.

The will acts in several ways. First it is that
quality in us that enables us to choose. Each has a will
of his own; we can select what we will do and what we
will be. To be able to choose is what constitutes individuality. The soil cannot choose what seed shall be
planted in it. The earth cannot choose whether it shall
spin about the sun. But we can choose what words we
shall say, what thoughts we shall think, what work we
shall do, or leave undone. Nor do we move in a fixed
orbit. We can choose what course we shall pursue,
what friends we shall cultivate, what causes we shall
support. It is a glorious morning exercise to select
wisely the path we shall follow today.

Having chosen, we also have the power to execute.

The will does not create but it is that attitude of mind that holds us to our desire until it is created for us. Plans may go wrong, the belt may slip on the pulley,— but the will swings things again into line. Friends may falter; the will wins them back. Individual plans may fail, but not the Great Plan, the Great Purpose for which we strive. No matter how many times some weakness shows, the will binds up the broken parts and pushes on to the end. The will holds on to life after the physician gives up. It "carries on" after hope has departed. It goes "over the top" and wrests victory from defeat. We *can* because we *think* we can.

The will also is a magnetic force. It enables an Alexander or a Caesar to make world empire; a Washington or a Lincoln to make men free. Your will exercises a subtle charm; your eager purpose sets men to working for you. Fortune smiles upon the man who dares. It favors the brave. Would you win men's respect? Then show them a great purpose. Would you compel circumstances to do your bidding? Then resolve this hour to be master today of self and circumstances.

> "You will be what you will to be;
>   Let failure find her false content
> In that poor word environment;
>   But *spirit* scorns it and is free:
> It masters time; it conquers space;
>   It cows that boastful trickster, chance,
> And bids the tyrant circumstance
>   Uncrown and fill a servant's place."

REALIZATION.

I am receptive to the highest wisdom today so that I choose only that which is best for me and others. I now choose this course (mention it), I will go on to its fulfilment. I do not fear men or conditions today. Circumstances have no power over me. I make circumstances. I am master of my fate. I am free to will and to do. I feel the God-power acting in me. I breathe the finer forces. My firm will is a magnet. It draws to me my good. It attracts and holds friends for me. I have a courageous soul, I am open to the highest truth, and I show only the greatest wisdom in my affairs. I play my part today with all the power of a mind conscious of its infinite strength and filled with the divine love and wisdom. I have the will to win. I can because God can.

LESSON XXVII.

CREATING ATMOSPHERES, AND PROSPERITY.

WE make our own heaven and our own hell through the conscious or unconscious use of the Law. We do it by the thoughts we think and the attitude we assume. For the Great Law receives our mental impression and brings out into form the ideas of our mind. We are not, therefore, the creatures of some chance environment or circumstances. There is something in us that attracts us to them and them to us. If it were not so we would move out of them. Do not complain about the world you live in. It is a reflection of your own thought. Do not blame others. Seek the cause in your own thinking. Ask, "What is it that brought me here? What was my thought of failure that produced this?" Then decide on the environment and circumstance you desire and mentally see yourself in your new surroundings. Then you are on the road to attainment, and your changes will begin to take place naturally from *within*. Your good does not come from without. The sooner you learn that you cannot expect someone else to hand it to you the better off you will be. You cannot change the un pleasant to the pleasant by a mere change of place.

We are all surrounded by the atmosphere that most

158

corresponds to our mental mood. So soon as we change our mood, we shall find ourselves in better conditions. Every person and every place is surrounded by an impalpable atmosphere which people feel even when they don't know what it is that affects them. Before the writer had learned these great truths, he spent a night with a physician in whose house many operations were performed for appendicitis. The atmosphere was so strong of this fear that he caught the contagion of thought, and later was operated on to have the thought cut out. Unless our mind is very positive, we become susceptible to the atmospheres about us. We must be careful not to attract ourselves to negative mental atmospheres, and should we find ourselves at any time open to negative influence, we must assume at once a positive attitude and declare ourselves surperior to it. Disease often comes by some impression from without which we harbor; after a while the thought develops like the seed and grows from within. *It can never become a disease for us until we accept it, either consciously or by tacit agreement to the race suggestion, and allow it to grow from within.*

Many places have strongly suggestive atmospheres. Some business places radiate good will and success. Others are full of a feeling of failure and general despair. Enter some atmospheres and you are seized with the desire to laugh and dance and sing. Go into others and you feel like weeping. Contact people who are constantly thinking along the lines of music and you will experience a new interest in it. Contact literary men and women and you will feel a desire to create. One woman bought a new house, and soon found herself desiring to write, although she had never shown any interest before in that direction. Later she discovered that an author had lived there and used one of the rooms as her study.

At one time we had a metaphysical sanitorium. We bought a large house and advertised for patients. At first few came, although we were widely known. One day a patient of ours who lived in the city and came for daily treatment was late for her appointment. On asking her the reason why, we found she had been sitting for an hour in the park, feeling that something kept her from approaching the house. We began to make inquiries and found the house had been previously used as a private hospital, and many patients had been sick or died there. We accordingly went through all the rooms of the house and treated them all for the atmosphere of peace and faith, mentally filling them with patients. In a short time all the rooms in the house were filled and our business was thereafter always a success.

People are very sensitive to atmospheres and can tell very well what others think of them though no words pass between them. Jesus was like that and was able to tell Simon the general trend of his thought. He said in effect, "Simon you are condemning and criticising me for my kindly attitude toward this woman."

And then He showed him that He was quite in-different to his opinion. Jesus, in turn, radiated an atmosphere so full of good will and healing power that people were healed by contact with His atmosphere or as some call it, His aura. This occurred in the case of the woman who touched Him in the crowd. "Virtue flowed out of Him." That is, vir or life energy, radi-ated from Him.

The chief charm of personality lies in the power of the individual to radiate a certain magnetic influence just as the sun radiates light and heat. The great leaders of history seem almost to have been charged with electricity, so powerful was the magnetic circle with which they were surrounded. Dr. Newell Dwight Hillis calls attention to this in a remarkable essay on "The Contagion of Character." He says: "Froude exhibits Julius Caesar drawing men unto him as a magnet draws particles of iron and steel. The rude Roman soldiers could no more escape the magnetic presence of their general than they could dodge the gravity of the earth. That most interesting writer, Hammerton, was deeply impressed by the state-ment that Napoleon's hand-grip was like a powerful electric shock." American history affords us striking illustrations in such men as George Washington, John Paul Jones, Philip Sheridan famous for the brilliant episode at Cedar Creek, Abraham Lincoln, both as citizen and as president. In every walk of life we encounter men unusually charged with a dynamic power which strangely affects us.

Spiritual Radiations.

Such an atmosphere may be either of physical, mental or spiritual origin, or may combine the elements of all. It has always been most remarkable in the most spiritual men. The atmosphere of such men is vibrant with healing energy that is often very astonishing. Next to Jesus, the disciples most evidenced this healing power, being most rarely spiritual or else most completely turning their energies in this direction. Bernard of Clairveaux is a type of the medieval saint who performed some really wonderful and undoubtedly authentic cures in this same manner. His spiritual aroma was exceedingly powerful and wrought many cures.

The Atmosphere of Places.

The presence of such characters often endows places or localities with a subtle atmosphere most conducive to health. Around these places the health-thought lingers. Faith here has its most perfect works. One naturally thinks at once of the town of Lourdes in France. In a grotto here, the Virgin Mary is accredited with having appeared to a peasant maid in 1858. Later on a church was erected over the grotto and unnumbered thousands have come to drink of the waters, to pray and be healed of their diseases and weaknesses. A great collection of canes and crutches evidence mutely to the fact of some of the cures.

Some of the most interesting experiments ever made by scientists were those of the photography of thought atmospheres by the Frenchman, Dr. Baraduc. He secured a photograph of the atmosphere of this very place, showing the presence of white lights or thought centers rising above those who came in faith for heal ing and filling the room.

In Quebec the Church of St. Anne de Beaupré has been the scene of similar healings through faith and prayer. While doubtless many cures recorded have been only temporary or apparent, due to causes easily explained, yet the fact remains that the atmosphere or thought-aroma of the place is highly charged with healing power, and thousands are healed therein.

It becomes very evident therefore that thoughts are things and that *our world is the world of our own choosing and making.* Since we have the power to create the atmosphere by which we are surrounded we should "guard our hearts with diligence, for out of it are the issues of life."

We should recognize, too, that we tend to draw to us and to draw ourselves to the circumstances and people most like ourselves and our thought. If, therefore, you do not like your present circumstances, change your way of thinking. Give conscious thought to this subject and begin to create a new heaven and a new earth for yourself.

REALIZATION.

I make my own heaven today. This day is what I make it and my world is what I make it. Today I am blessed because I bless: I am prospered because I believe in my prosperity. I have friends because I am one. I have love because I love. (If your business is not prosperous go into your store and bless it.) This place is my place. It is the reflection of my thought. No other has any power over this place to give it an idea of failure. There cannot be any lingering thought of failure here. This place is full of the atmosphere of success and good-will. Everybody who comes here is optimistic and prosperous. I attract business and success. I inspire people with confidence. I radiate the subtle atmosphere of success. People who come in here feel it. I have a constant attitude of faith toward my business. I do not think about failure, but only of success. I shall forget what happened yesterday and before, if it was not success. I establish a new standard for this place. (Realize that it will do no great good for you to say it and not mean it. And it will do no great good for you to mean it only for the time you are saying it. Hold this mental attitude all day. Hold it every day until the atmosphere is created and you are a success in visible expression. Put out your best efforts and *act* in such a way that people will *feel* that everything is all right. Bankers have been known to stop a run on the bank when things were bad from a material standpoint, just by holding a lofty mental attitude and giving confidence to their patrons. I have known people to succeed in the eleventh hour. Be one of them.)

Go on then, blessing your place all day. If it is the

home and there is inharmony there, treat it in the same way, and say:—

This house is the house of my spirit and the home of my heart. It cannot have inharmony for I am harmony and love and I draw only love here. Everyone in this house is thoughtful, kind and considerate. I have faith in everybody here and my faith is justified. I am now conscious of a new mental attitude and no one coming into this home can fail to notice it. All is harmony and everything is delightful.

One should think this truth each day until results are secured. And never fail to give thanks that your faith has found its place in the Cosmic Creative Mind and that it is being done unto you as you think.

LESSON XXVIII.

THE PERSONAL SPIRIT.

THE enlarging views of God have disturbed many because they have feared to lose the personality of the Divine Presence. They have thought that they must make a choice between God without law and law without God, and have chosen the former. As a matter of fact no such choice is necessary or possible. God must be accepted *with* law since there can be no separation. And in making this statement we are not differing from the intelligent thought of the leaders of the orthodox church, for advanced theologians, like the late William Clarke or Washington Gladden, have been for many years teaching the church to enlarge its concept of God away from the limitations of human personality. We ought no longer to think of Spirit in terms of form but rather of feeling. Our own real nature is the *inner quality* of our life with its infinite capacity, and we ought to learn to think of God as the infinite extension of the best in us without the limitations of individuality. Thus we shall recognize Him as the All of Life, Love, and Wisdom, and not as a person in the ordinary sense. By personality is meant of necessity a mind apart from some other. One can be a person only by being distinct from some other. This is impossible with God since He is **All** and "the

Lord thy God is *one* God."' To conceive of God *as a person* is to recognize *two* powers in the universe; God or Good, and some other who is Not God and not good, and is therefore evil. Then an inevitable conflict of wills must result in which two infinite powers strive with each other for mastery; chaos would be the result and the cosmos would be reduced to zero. Good and evil would be of equal power and reality and it would be useless to strive against nature in the hope of overcoming evil. Since God is infinite it is impossible for Him to be limited by an opposing power; since He is Truth and Truth is *that which is,* the only conceivable opposite to God is that *which is not.* "Beside Me there is none other."

We must therefore think of God in other terms than that of the ordinary concept of personality. The ancients found this in the law itself, saying, "Verily the Law is a Person," for they found that the Law reflected their faith with infinite exactness. If one looks to the Law with thoughts of faith and love, he finds a response in it to his mood. If he looks with hate and skepticism into his universe, it appears tragic to him. This is why Jesus spoke of it as the Father giving bread to His children because they ask bread; and again as the adversary, casting the debtor into prison until he pays the utmost farthing. To those whose faith turns heavenward expecting good, it comes; to those who think in terms of limitation and fear and want the law becomes the adversary. It is therefore like a person, said the Jewish rabbis, for it reflects our moods with utmost exactness.

Accordingly if one looks at his universe with faith, it will justify his confidence; if he gives his heart in adoring love to the Divine Mind, It gives back measure for measure of Its own divine nature. Thus with the poet we may say,

> "Speak to Him thou, for He heareth,
>   And spirit with Spirit can meet,
> Closer is He than breathing,
>   Nearer than hands or feet."

Thus the Infinite acts through Its law with all the intelligence of Its nature reflecting to us with absolute accuracy whatever mood or feeling we display toward It. According to the nature of our faith it is done unto us. This removes the element of *chance* from the response God makes to our prayers. For God is thus bound to act through law and not through individual choices of will. To believe that God acts through individual choices of will is to give Him personality; and He *may* answer our prayer or may not, giving or withholding arbitrarily. If God acts by choice of will rather than by law, it is useless to pray for we have no way to be sure of anything He will do.

But He acts by law; and we may, therefore, perceive that the issue lies with us as to what we shall receive. If we obey the law it will be our servant and do what we ask it. "Ask and ye shall receive, seek and ye shall find." God acts *through* law to give "according' to your faith."

Nor does this rob God of freedom to act nor the *attributes* of personality. We may be sure there are no *attributes* in the Son which are not inherited from the Father.

Man is self-conscious and self-directing; so is God. He is not, like man, conscious of Himself as individual or apart from another, but He is conscious of Being— He is conscious of feeling and thinking. He is con scious of joy and love and creative power. He experi ences states of consciousness which constitutes being.

Again, He is *self-directing*. He has the power of selecting as to how, when, and where He will act. He starts a universe when He will, and places it where He will. Planets are born at different times, some being so old that the light has gone out from their sun; others being so new that their flickering youthful light has hardly had time to reach us through the immense diffusion of space. But having chosen, Creative Mind ever *acts by law* and science itself is merely the systematic investigation of God's *orderly* way of working. All discoveries of the highest intellect confirm the law of God's activity. And this is as true of the "natural law in the spiritual world" as elsewhere. "All's love, yet all's law," says Browning.

Yet "He that made the ear, shall He not hear?" "He that made the eye, shall He not see?" Infinite in power, perfect in wisdom, tender in love, God becomes to those who seek Him in simple childlike faith, the

Father "Who forgiveth all thine iniquities, Who healeth all thy diseases, Who crowneth thee with loving kindness and tender mercies, Who satisfieth thy mouth with good things so that thy youth is renewed like the eagle's."

REALIZATION.

To realize the presence of the Personal Spirit is to find channels of power for the Word in all our affairs. We must learn to perceive God as the Father, forever standing at the doorway of His house to welcome the returning prodigal.

To realize the presence, it is essential to employ heart and mind and will. We must use the mind and will to swing back the door on its rusty hinges. This can be done in this way—a way I have found very helpful. We begin by talking to ourselves something like this:

I am now entering into the secret Presence; I am coming into touch with All-That-Is. The world is shut out. I am shut in, in the temple of my own soul. Life and love and peace and God are all about me. In Him I live and move and have my being. Every breath I breathe is the breath of the spirit. I am drinking of the water of life freely. The pure clear stream of love divine is flowing through my body like a current, carrying away all impure and selfish thoughts, all weakness, all evil, all meanness, all sin. It cleanses me thoroughly in body and in mind and washes away all my sin. There is left now nothing but purity and love. The river of God fills me. From within me flow springs of living water. The life of God is in me. The love of God fills me. The peace of God holds me. Fear and worry and all that is unlike God, has gone away from me. I am filled with the love of God. God is here. Then we may continue by repeating the Twenty-third or Sixty-first Psalm, or some poem that suggests the Divine Presence.

LESSON XXIX.

INTUITION AND IDEATION.

THE fine responsiveness of the law, which we have observed in the chapter on the Personal Spirit, appeals to the highest instincts in us. It fills us at once with gratitude and confidence. We realize that "no good thing will He withhold from them that walk uprightly," and that if we will place ourselves under the guidance of the Spirit, "He will teach us all things and guide us in the way of truth." For we need to realize this, that God is more than His law, though He work through law; and that if He has intelligence enough to bring to pass those things for which we pray, He also has the capacity to "teach us *how* to pray." In other words, we find God acting *through the law* as our invisible guide, as we noted in the fourth part of the law in Lesson II.

If the law is infinitely responsive, it must be as quick to answer us in response to a call for *wisdom* and *guidance* as to give us those *things* for which we ask. The way this is accomplished is for us to assume toward the law the attitude of receptivity for the wisdom we need. We must recognize that Divine Wisdom knows just what course it is best for us to pursue under given circumstances; and we may therefore turn to it with perfect confidence, while sitting

172

quietly in the silence and making conscious unity with
the Spirit of All Wisdom. Recognize that in essential
nature "the Father and I are one." There is no
separtion in this one wisdom; therefore the knowledge
of truth is in you now. "As the Father hath inherent
life in Himself, so hath He given it to the son to
have life in himself"; this life is the divine intelligence
in you, universal and knowing all the particulars of
the case in point. But this divine wisdom is the undifferentiated of all knowledge and what you desire
is that it shall differentiate its wisdom through you to
the particular application in hand. You may therefore say, "Infinite wisdom now leads me and directs
me as to the course which I should follow." Then you
may remain for a while in the silence and come forth
with expectancy to the tasks before you. You will go
to work making your decisions on the basis of your
good judgment, knowing that you cannot go wrong;
and that if you should be on the point of false judgments something will rise in you as an instinct to tell
you that this course is wrong. That is the voice of
the intuitions upon which you have called. Heed it
and go on without fear along the path that will be
pointed out to you.

It is here that a true spirituality will count. And by
spirituality we mean a consciousness of ultimate
reality and the presence of Spirit, a deep feeling of the
union of your own mind with the Divine. These are
qualities which are developed by practice. The student
of psychology and physiology knows that there are

brain-centers and nerve-systems especially, adapted to
the influx of pure ideas from the universal and their
method of reaching the objective mind by which we
cognize and act upon them.   This is carefully explained in Chapter 14 of the Edinburgh Lectures by
Judge Troward and the student may profitably read
that chapter.   The point which I wish to make plain
is that if we are to depend upon the intuitions we
must follow the law of intuitions and place ourselves
in the utmost harmony with Spirit.   As Spirit is, above
all, *Feeling,* we shall find that our intuitions will be
largely a matter of feeling; and yet after a time we can
act upon them with certainty for the impressions will
be deep enough to form a sure guide for us.   At the
same time we must be sure that *intuitions* and mere
impressions are not confounded in our thought.   Many
people are constantly getting impressions which are
merely the vagrant thoughts of other minds, race
concepts, or fears and similar thoughts rising out of
the subconscious where they have been embedded.
Large numbers of people get these impressions as
psychic experiences and they should be carefully
guarded against, for they often bring inharmony and
worse.   A good criterion to follow is as to whether
the impression is directly along the line for which we
have been seeking guidance.   If not, it is probably not
an intuition.   Again, we should seek to note the *first*
impression as most dependable.   We often meet people
who on first approach do not appeal to us.   Later we
get over this feeling, but there comes a time when our

first impression is proven to have been correct. The reason for this is that the subjective self is far more impressionable than the objective and is in touch with a wider field of knowledge.

Many have found it a valuable practice upon retiring to bed at night to state that they will receive direction from Infinite Wisdom along a given line. Then, on waking, they note their first thoughts about the matter in hand and find that if they follow the intuitions thus given that they do not go wrong. I have always found this to be true in my own experience, that if I seek direction on retiring and then subsequently act on my judgment at the time the business in hand requires, that my affairs have always gone well. In this connection one might well read the story of Jesus' intuitions and those of Brother Lawrence, the medieval saint.

IDEATION.

The intuitions can also be followed in another important respect, and that is in relation to the formation of the idea or concept which we wish to have embodied through the activity of the Law. We have already learned that the law works on the model, idea, or image which we reflect into it. Now it often happens that our ideas may be limited and our understanding of the thing necessary or expedient for us to do or have at a given time may be too insecure for us to mould it into mental form. In such case, we must recognize that if we do not know the best thing to have, there is a spirit in us that *does* know, and we may therefore depend on it.   In this connection I urge the student to study my book "Being and Becoming" which fully explains this principle.   It is sufficient here to say that if our motives are high and pure and our faith steadfast, it is not necessary for us to have a perfect image so far as the objective mind is concerned.   There is a mind in us that does know just what is best and this mind can hold up to the Law the *idea* of what we want; then the intuitions and the Creative Mind alike work upon our problem to bring forth what will be best for us.   This is not a mere saying, "Thy will be done whether it is mine or not." It is not mere quiescence and letting things go.   It is quite other than that; it is *expecting something to happen along a definite line for you in the best way.* You may not know the *form* the desired good will take, but you do have now a definite idea.

You realize that Spirit itself is Idea and that what you want is the embodied idea; and often, when you make a demonstration, you find that Spirit, which "knows what things ye have need of before ye them," has embodied the idea in the answer to your realization although it takes a different *form* from what you had anticipated.

Nor need we fear to trust our desired good to the Law.   Infinite Intelligence will work upon it to bring it forth in the finest form.   Spirit itself is formative; it is the power that conceived a universe, dreamed a rose, and thought man into form.   It had no pattern for the moulding of its ideas into form. But it knew how to embody them; and, as it is eternally creative, it will body forth your idea whether it be an invention no one else has ever conceived, a melody never before sung, or a motif in art never before breathed into the beauty of color.

Here genius has its incubus, all invention its birth, all art its inspiration, all wisdom its source. Dare to launch out on life's uncharted sea, for in you the Great Pilot, the Great Adventurer, the Great Poet, the Great Inventor, the Great Musician, the Great Artist is making Its great quest for individual experience. Genius springs from the soul that dares to drink at the fountains of inspiration in the garden of God. Thus Spirit helps us to conceive and bring into birth the highest we can desire. It gives to us *"above* all we ask or think."

REALIZATION.

I now have faith in the inner power of spirit working through me. I trust in the inner wisdom. This wisdom is not mine, neither is it intelligence apart from me: it is God in me. I trust in the divine illumination of my own soul in which I am one with the Father. If I do not yet know objectively, there is that in me that does know. (Now bring your feeling of this truth up to the highest point and then say: I desire and will receive guidance along this line. I shall be told what course it is best for me to follow. Then rest in quiet expectation that something will occur which will enable you to make a choice of the right thing. Then go about your daily work with perfect faith that at the right time Spirit will show you what to do and guide you into the best things. If you have proceeded in the right way, you will find that you will now *know in your heart* that *this* is the thing you should do or have. Having been instructed as to the best course to follow or the best thing to have, go to work to realize it in the same way as for any other "realization.")

(When it comes to the "demonstration" of health, the healer will realize that it is not necessary that we shall know how the internal organ should appear, nor what shape it will have. There is in us That that does know, and if we hold mentally to perfection in thought, each organ of the body will answer with a correspondence in form.

In manifesting prosperity, the same rule will hold. Therefore declare your faith in the perfect intelligence of the Law, put forth the idea in thought and then *let the Supreme Intelligence in you find the best way* to accomplish it for you. The mind in you that formulates and the mind that executes are **One**; and so the thought must become the thing, or, your word be made flesh.)

I am conscious of the creative activity of the Divine Intelligence acting for me along this line and I give thanks that it is done unto me even as I will.

LESSON XXX.

ULTIMATE REALITY AND THE FATHER HOOD OF GOD.

LAW is everywhere yet law is not all. Since law is a *way* of *working,* there must be That which works that way. The student is to be warned against too great emphasis upon the Law, lest he make the Law of Cause and Effect his God rather than That which is neither cause nor effect. And again we must be careful lest in simplifying our teaching to a few fixed principles, we conceive these principles to be the all or ultimate. Since Law is the activity of a principle, we must realize that there must be a principle to act. There is no act without the actor; no song without the singer; no art without the artist. God is the Great Actor, the Lofty Musician, the Supreme Artist. As each form of art depends on the spirit of the artist, so each form or law of creation must depend on the Spirit or Creator. We learn from this that when we use the law we are not manipulating God.

We must, therefore, learn to think back of the visible to the invisible, back of the limited to the absolute. In a book of this kind we can only point the way. The study of the Absolute is essential and is the work of the advanced student. It is only by deduction, axiomatic and abstract reasoning that we can at all penetrate the mystery of the Absolute, save by feeling. I hope some day to issue a book on this subject. Meanwhile I wish to point out a general direction our thought should take. To know the Law and to feel that, therefore, we know all is very dangerous. It may lead to wrong mental practice and ultimate failure. We must therefore constantly strive to realize the *Spirit that underlies the Law*, to identify ourselves with it, to perceive the living presence of the Absolute, to discover not merely impersonality in the law but to find in it the activity of Person. Thus we must learn to think deeply for we have on the one hand the danger of materialism in the use of an impersonal law, and on the other the danger of establishing an impossible personality as our thought of God.

Will the student therefore realize that what we have already learned is not Truth *per se* but is about Truth? Will you not therefore constantly apply yourself to the realization of the Absolute? Back of the law there still stands the Indivisible; the Inscrutable; the Changeless; the Eternal; the Unalterably Perfect; the Complete; the Universal; Truth unreasoned; First Principle; the All; the Incomparable; the Undifferentiate of life, love and wisdom; in short the Exhaustless Storehouse of All-That-Is, Spirit, Power-to-Become; the Absolute.

These are the names of God conceived by the intellect; but back of them is the Nameless Name, the Un spoken Word. Just as no one has ever seen a star but only the vibration of light that has been streaming from it perhaps for thousands of years, so no man has perceived God directly but only through mental concepts. Reason which is not absolute must posit God or that which is absolute. Says the Apostle John, "No man hath seen God at any time; the only begotten Son, Who is in the bosom of the Father, He hath *declared* Him." Reason can never comprehend God, but it can declare Him. Reason proves Him to be all, since we can discover no quality such as life, love, wisdom, supply, beauty which does not come from a source inexhaustible; and no matter how far back we go in the series, still we find a cause until reason moves from cause to Causeless Cause, or All; yet however much God may be grasped by the understanding, still He remains the Eternal Mystery. Only by faith can He be apprehended. As we are all begotten of the only God, which is the correct translation of monogenes, (not the "only begotten") we "declare God." But how?

IN MAN, THE ABSOLUTE.

There is in man himself the undiscovered country of the absolute. In man is that which is indivisible, inscrutable, changless, eternal, perfect, complete and power-to-manifest. There is in man that out of which all things proceed. No limitation has ever been discovered to the power of life, love, and wisdom in man. However much he displays these Godlike powers, he still retains the capacity for more of the same thing. No boundaries can be set to his capacity. Reason has its limitations, but the *capacity of being* has no limitations.

Since, then, in God is the limitless, and in man is the limitless, and since in both the potential power is of the same nature, then both are one. This is the divine unity.

Or we may come to the same conclusion in another way: God is Truth and Truth is all. Besides Truth there is nothing. If we are to be at all, we must be at one with this Truth or All. Again since Truth is a unity—for it is all—then there is that about us which is universal. Thus man contacts the absolute in all respects and by knowing himself can know God. Yet no man fully knows his own nature, and what we think and feel is not our self. Above all thinking, feeling, and sensation is that eternal element, the self. Above poverty, want, fear, pain, unhappiness, is that which is all, divine, unchanging, eternal, absolute. But we can only know this higher self by what it does. Therefore we may say both of the self and God, that they are the Great Mystery of Being.

Who Is God?

Who then is God? We can think of God in other terms than the intelligence, ever engaged in answering the prayers of the sick, poor, and unhappy; constantly busying itself with filling the orders for our "demonstrations." God dwells in a light unapproachable.

His Law does His work. Wrapped in the robes of His own being, the eternal God is eternal realization of being. Constantly experiencing states of consciousness (which is being), God forever delights in harmonies and glories of the Creative Mind. He glories alike in the being and the making. Having the power to hear and the infinite thought of harmony, God thrills to the ecstasies of the eternal music of the universe, visible and invisible   Soft melodies delight Him, grand strains of song celestial gladden Him with their sweet melodies. Orchestras supernal forever peal forth their thrilling notes engaging and satisfying with their perfect rhythm.

But even as God dreams these harmonies celestial, the Great Law of His being bodies them forth into the music of the spheres, the rippling song of the brook, and the note of the nightingale.

And while music delights the Soul-of-All, His heart is throbbing with the divine ecstasy of love. He is feeling the impulses of affection. Thrill on thrill in richest feeling passes through His gladdened heart. And the Great Law bodies it forth into beauties of sunrise and sunset, of starry vaults of heaven, of human hearts all-glorified in lovers; betrothals, mothers, babes, mating-things from atoms up to man.

Thoughts of the Infinite go forth to create with all the joy of thinking things new. As one in luxuriant ease lies upon a bed of boughs upon some mountain height and, in the sense of well-being, love, life, and supply, gazes in uplifted wonder upon the earth and sea and sky and breathes a sigh of hushed and sweet contentment, so God lives within His universe and joys in His being and making.

Thus God is All and observes all. No splendid sun drives bravely through the pathway of the sky, singing as it runs, but God sees and hears. He is in the flashing of the comet and the flicker of the star.

Thus the birth and growth of every wild thing, the wee budding of the woodland violet, the grub that churns the earth, the bird that springs into the sky, are all in the mind of God, and God is in them all.

If then, not a sparrow can fall to the ground but your heavenly Father seeth it, if He feeds the ravens, shall man who shares His life, go unseen and unsatisfied? Rather should we perceive ourselves as the center of God's choice activity. Rather should we see that when we allow Him to so appear to us, He is the Good Shepherd leading us in green pastures and beside the still waters where He restores our souls. Rather should we see in God, the Father Who goes forth to meet the returning Prodigal and puts on his finger the ring of His affection. And in glorified realization we should enter into the secret place of the Most High where we may abide under the shadow of the Almighty. We should learn to listen to the music of the world and hear in Nature the voice of God. In the deeper silences of our soul we, too, should thrill to celestial harmonies; we too, should feel deeply the throbbing joy of well-being and love unaffected. Song of the soul, sing in my heart; joy of the world, thrill through my being. Now do I bow down and worship, I kneel before the Lord and say, "My Father Who art in heaven, hallowed be Thy name; Thy kingdom come, Thy will be done in me."

REALIZATION.

There is but one realization for the Absolute. "Be still and know that I am God."

LESSON XXXI.

THE SUPREME AFFIRMATION.

THE first principle of the law is that it produces for us just what we think. It becomes to us just what we become to it. If we assume an attitude of love and harmony toward the universe, it becomes Mother Nature to us. If we look upon it as hard and cruel, it becomes to us inexorable fate. *The law brings into form what we think.* While this seems a hard saying when we think of all the ills that come to us, yet the thoughtful mind would not have it otherwise; for if our wrong thoughts and attitudes of mind bring distress, then our right thoughts will bring us joy and supply. This is the dependableness of the law. The law never changes; we alone change. The law is invariable; we alone are variable. The law is like the current of electricity; it is always the same power, but we may apply to it the variable factor of the instrument we use, and draw from it either light, or heat, or power.

Now *the affirmation, when rightly used and understood, is simply the statement of the attitude you assume toward the law.* It is to say to yourself, "I am receptive to this particular thing from Divine Mind. I am at one with It on this point." God is more ready to give than we are to receive, but He cannot give until we assume the attitude of receptivity. "Ask and ye shall receive; seek, and ye shall find." The great seekers are the great finders. This is faith which launches out on the unknown sea and finds the undiscovered country. The *supreme* affirmation is therefore the *supreme attitude of mind* toward the law. It is the highest statement. It is faith, for faith is a confident attitude of expectancy of the thing you are seeking.

The question then arises as to what is the highest attitude of mind. And the answer is that there is no attitude of mind so high as the conscious recognition of the spiritual reality of being. To be conscious of one's self as spirit; to be conscious of the universe as thought in form (Lesson VIII) and to be conscious of thought as the ruling power over all things, this is supreme. That is why all statements of being begin with God as all; man as His child, sharing His nature and resources; and the necessary conclusion that all power is therefore given unto man in heaven and on earth.

The *supreme attitude, we say, is the consciousness of being.* It is the consciousness of *that which is.* Jesus said, "God is spirit and they which worship Him must worship Him in spirit and in truth." That God is spirit is not something to be proven by the intellect and reason; it is rather something that we intuitively feel to be true. The supreme attitude is therefore not some intellectual proof of being, but is rather a feeling of reality. It is to know in one's heart that what we desire is ours so soon as we are ready to appropriate it. It is to realize that we do not have to *make* things; we only have to "let them be." What we desire exists in the Divine Mind the moment we desire it. In spirit it already is a reality and by the process of materialization it will soon pass into form and come into our hands. Thus our "word is made flesh and dwells among us." Thus we "know the truth and the Truth of itself makes us free." We do not have to make our good, but we must put it up to the Creative Mind and Law to make it for us.

Now since the law assumes toward us the attitude we assume toward it, we perceive that the stronger our conviction of our own life-essence or being is felt by us, the stronger will that thought be impressed on Creative Mind. Then since Creative Mind becomes to us just what we become to It, we find It pouring back into us increasing measures of its own life and being. As soon as we reflect into it the thought of life, It becomes increasing power-to-live to us. If we re-, fleet into it the thought of love, it becomes increasing lovingness to us. The heart that is closest to God always feels the greater power of His love. The closer we get to Him the closer He becomes to us. New beauties dawn on our vision. New songs sing forth from heaven. New joys await us. Higher emotions become possible. The spiritual mind sees visions celestial where the gross mind sees nothing; hears voices in nature where the materialist hears sounds. As we draw nearer to Spirit, Spirit draws nearer to us.

> "And behind the dim unknown
> Standeth God within the shadows
> Keeping watch above His own."

The supreme affirmation, therefore, is a statement of being—"I am." When Moses asks, "Whom shall I tell the children of Israel that you are?" the Voice says, "**I Am That I Am.**" I am the Absolute-of-All-That-**Is.** I am pure being. I am the Nameless Name. I am the Proofless Proof. I am that which is. */ The supreme affirmation is the realization of the self as identified with Pure Being or God.* I am at one with the All. I am. I am being. I am spirit. I am life. I am substance.

I am that which was in the beginning, is now, and ever shall be. I am not that which was made. I exist from eternity to eternity. I am the life more abundant. I am a center of the activity of Divine Mind. I am a point of consciousness in the All-Mind. I am one with the Infinite. I and the Father are one. /

Assuming this attitude toward the Divine Mind is to cause it to assume toward you a more intimate attitude. You become a still more intensified center of consciousness because you draw around you still greater resources of Mind. / Just as the botanist's study and thought upon a flower reveals its greater beauty and symmetry, so that he knows more about the flower than another person, and accumulates still more knowledge about flowers by attracting information, so we accumulate greater resources of wisdom, life, and love, and supply by assuming a more intimate attitude toward them and their source.

Not only life and love are thus realized in heightened measure, but also supply. For in the realm of spirit or Divine Mind from which all things spring, the *things* we want are spiritual substance or thought; and when the thought comes forth into form, it still exists *within the form.* The thought is, in fact, an individual, though not self-conscious, entity. We may call it the soul of the thing. The soul is the intelligence which exists within the form and sustains it. The length of the life of the form or thing depends on the power with which the thought in it has been endowed. It is by the recognition that there is a thought-entity, soul, or intelligence within Nature and all her manifestations and in all "things" that we can control our world and environment; for the superior and *conscious* intelligence in us can dominate the lower world of intelligence unconscious of itself.

We can therefore attract the thing we want by realizing that the substance of which it is composed and the intelligence by which it is sustained is one and the same with the real essence of our own nature. We *identify* our life with the life or thought that sustains the thing; so that the supreme affirmation is the *assertion that we, and thought, and thing are one,* accompanied with the deep feeling of the truth of

our statement. It is to say and *feel,* "I am supply. I am riches. My thought is my wealth and my riches when I identify it with the thought of Spirit"

This is the reason, therefore, that we frequently say, "I am."

> "One sits behind the awful change
> And calmly says, 'I am.'
> Above the sky, though storm clouds fly,
> Though Justice bleed, and peoples die
> While nations follow the great lie,
> I am and still I am.
>
> The sun shall rise; the grass shall grow,
> The clouds across the sky shall go,
> The ancient rivers still shall flow,
> I am and still I am."*

REALIZATION.

Infinite Life, I live and breath in Thee. I am Thine. I am Thy life made manifest. I am Thy center of self-realization. I am Thy love come forth to form. I am Thy great adventure into individuality. I, **too,** am love. I, **too,** am life. I, too, am peace. I, **too,** am the nameless substance. I, too, am spirit. I am life abundant. I am that which is. I am undying substance. I cannot die, for I am life. I cannot be sick for I am health. I cannot be unhappy, for I am **joy.**

---

*Edwin Davies Schoonmaker in *Nautilis,* January, 1918.

I turn from all that is negative that I may realize the great affirmative. I am. I am. I am. Why should I fear? I am. No danger can come to me. I am. I am spirit and I am life. I cannot be lost for I am in the Divine Mind. I cannot stray, for Thou art everywhere. I am. Let me rest in the calm and peace today, and when problems vex and things get out of place let me enter into the secret place of the Most High, let me bide a while under the shadow of the Almighty. I am; and still I am. In the secret place of my heart all is peace and all is quiet. There are no storms here. I am; and still I am.

Part II

TREATMENTS OR REALIZATIONS.

FORMS FOR DEVELOPMENT OF CONSCIOUSNESS.

LESSON I.

THE USE OF FORMULAS.

THE student has now arrived at a point where he realizes that no one can give him a magic healing phrase or be his consciousness for him. He must himself know the truth if he is to be free. At the same time he has learned that it is legitimate for him to use every means possible for the development of consciousness. The object is to bring the mind to the point where we *know* that our word not only *can* produce results but that it *will* and *does now*. The more the metaphysician *feels* this, the more certain are his results. This feeling or consciousness may be arrived at in a variety of ways. One may read books, like the Bible, to inspire his faith. Or he may meditate on truth and God. Or he may pray worshipfully, or listen to inspiring music, or study the flower in the crannied wall.

"Flower in the crannied wall,
 I pluck you out of the crannies,
Hold you in my hand, little flower;
 If I could understand what you are,
Root and all, and all in all,
 I should know what God and man is."

Or he may read how someone else was healed of disease. Finally, he may take a form of treatment like the following and, holding it in thought, may rise to the point of consciousness where he knows that the truth is about to set him free; thus he makes the words of the treatment *his word* to the law and it is done unto him even as he wills.

Let us realize, therefore, that the following are merely forms; let us not use them as mere formalism, but as steps into consciousness. They are not "treatments" after all; they are realizations or perceptions of truth and reality. Most of them are written in the form of self-help, but they can be used in the perception of truth for others. In the Divine Mind in which we live, move, and have our being, the *ego* and the *alter ego* have no essential line of separation. What is true in your mind therefore must be true for your patient. As God is All, there is no such thing as dividing lines in spirit. Do not recognize such. So far as your patient is concerned, when he has agreed to receive your help, he has signified that he is willing that your consciousness should be his. He has made his mind impersonal to you that you may impress upon it just that character which you both wish it to assume. He is open and receptive to your word. The word therefore is in his mind the moment it is in yours, for it is spoken in spirit where time and space do not exist. Since space does not exist, there can be no divisibility in mind, and the moment the truth is realized in yourself it is realized in him.

This fact is so deserving of the utmost clearness that we may well dwell upon it. It is the recognition of the unity of truth. Truth must of necessity be all, since what is not truth is nothing, and all plus nothing equals all. This means therefore that truth cannot be divided because if we divide it into parts there must be something to separate it into the assumed parts—something must come between which is not truth to cause the separation. But the presence of the opposite of truth, or nothing, cannot cause any real division. Truth is therefore an essential unity.

We have already studied this all-important subject in the lesson on Mind. We there discovered the essential unity of Spirit, Mind, or Truth, and learned that it is a unit. All the power of the unit is concentrated at any given point at any time by our contacting it. Just as the electric bulb may draw on all the electric current and still not exhaust it, so we may draw on all there is in God by contacting Him at any point. For since there is no real point or place in *Spirit, It is fully present wherever we recognize It.* If the student has fully grasped this he will realize that when he sits in the silence to "treat" a patient

he is simply *realizing the whole truth* for the patient.
Then, as *truth is everywhere with all power,* whatever is true in the healer's mind must of necessity be
true in the patient's mind. Then, if the healer's realization is perfect, he has drawn on all the power there is
for the patient. So the Great Teacher rightly claimed,
"All power is given unto me in heaven and on earth."
If God is all, and I live in God, and make my conscious unity with Him, then *all* the power there is must
wait upon my word.

In giving a treatment therefore it is very essential
to make a conscious unity with your patient before you
speak the word. You must realize that you both are
spirit living in the One Mind, and that whatever is
true for you in that Mind must of necessity be true
of him. In actual practice you will find that after a
while you do not have to think of this *consciously* as
you already have the consciousness of this truth. The
experienced healer seldom argues with himself or the
patient, because he already knows; but he has had
to pass through the very stage you are now passing
through in the development of his consciousness, so
do not be ashamed to work out your thought mechan-
ically if necessary. But all the time try to *feel the
truth* as deeply as you can while you think or use the
following treatments.

In regard to speaking mentally to the patient, you
are at liberty to follow any method that will give you
the highest consciousness. If it seems to bring him
closer to you, you may mentally see him when he is

at a distance: if you wish you may say, "You are so and so." But the use of the second person, or "you," may lead you to feel a sense of separation, so be sure you do not feel such to be the case. In the end you will reach a point where all that is necessary will be to take the name of the patient, whether present or absent, and then enter the silence of the All Mind and declare that all is perfect wholeness, truth, life, love and supply. You will then speak the word, "Let it be done unto you, even as you will." That is all, and if you can realize this at once, the patient will be healed as soon as he receives. He may at once be receptive or it may take time for the word to manifest. That is not *your* concern. You have spoken your word and realized the truth. You have nothing to do with what follows. If the patient fails to respond, because of some subtle doubt or unwillingness, to receive your word, it is not your fault. Leave that to the Law.

The following realization (Lesson II) is suggested by my brother, Ernest S. Holmes, as a good method for the beginner,

LESSON II.

THE HEALING POWER OR HOW TO HELP OTHERS.

"FIRST center your thought in the spirit; that is, realize that in the spirit is all harmony and all peace. Realize this until you feel it all through you. Get a picture in your mind of perfect peace, hold it for some time, be grateful for it, repeat some helpful passages from the Bible. This puts you in touch with power. Now your mind is at peace and resting on the spirit for all, turn your mental attention to your patient, see in him the same thing that you have seen in yourself. Picture him as being perfect **Now.** **Know** that **Now** the power of the spirit which is in him is his perfect health and life. See this for him until you perfectly realize it in him. Now you may call him by name and tell him that he is made in the image and likeness of God, and that the spirit of truth is working in him and is completely restoring him to perfect health. Realize this for him for some time before you go on any further. Now continue and tell him that his life is spiritual and not subject to any condition but the spirit. Feel this with all the power that you have. See it with all the sight that you have. Do not get anxious or make hard work of it. Be perfectly calm, positive and natural in everything you do and say.

Remember that it is the spirit of truth that you embody, which is to do the work. This is the **Only** way that you can hope for good results. Now remind him that, as a child of God, he is being cared for by the Spirit of God; he is therefore full of faith in that power and he is receiving that power into his thought and into his life. See this and feel it for him, calmly, positively, and with absolute assurance. Now tell him that he is perfect and whole in his spiritual nature and that he will manifest it in his physical nature. Now give the power of the spirit the whole place for a few minutes, realizing that it is doing the work. Repeat the Lord's prayer slowly and with deep feeling. If you like, repeat several good thoughts from the Bible. Now give all into the keeping of the **All Father,** and rest in peace, for the work is done, as far as you are concerned. Hold this feeling of faith and wholeness for some time, and finish by saying: 'It Is Done through the power of the spirit and in the name of Christ.' '

LESSON III.

WHOM TO TREAT.

IN his first enthusiasm the eager finder of truth feels that he would like to heal the stripes of all the world. He has compassion on the multitude because they are as sheep without a shepherd. This is natural and right; for loving and compassionate interest in our fellowmen is an indispensible law of healing. But it must not lead to wrong practices. You do not have the right to treat everybody. To treat those who might regard your efforts as an inexcusable interference, is wrong. Just because it might do them good is not a sufficient reason. Unless the case is very exceptional, such treatments are a mental invasion of their volitional rights. It is mental suggestion, hypnotism, and malpractice. In all cases where the patient is mentally incompetent you have a perfect right to heal. This would include insanity, hallucination, cases of accident where the patient is unable to choose. In all cases where other people are in danger you have a right to give your help, and you will find that subjectively the patient is reaching out for help and therefore is receptive. In case someone near to you, as a member of the family, is violating the laws of life, you must study out for yourself how far you have a right to speak them into truth. If their acts bring distress to you, you may treat yourself that you are in harmonious surroundings and that all those who come near to you are self-controlled, considerate, and loving. This will cure most cases. If they speak harshly or act unkindly, you can declare the opposite. Say, "I see you loving, kind, and considerate," or make such other statement as appeals to you.

There will always be cases where you would like to help but at present cannot. You can declare that the way is opening up for you to speak the truth to them. You can by the silent word open up the pathway to their minds, but after it is open you must *let the truth make its own appeal.* You must not force its acceptance. To attempt it is to violate another's individuality. Inquisitions have been established, thousands have been burned at the stake, murders unnumbered have been committed, battles have been fought, nations have been drenched in blood, peoples have been exterminated and civilizations have been extinguished by the well-meant effort of religious zealots who sought to force other people to accept their truth. Let us not perpetuate the system. Let us have no established, systematized, dogmatized, orthodoxy of the truth. Let us emancipate the souls of men as well as their bodies. Had God desired conformity to the truth rather than individuality, He would have made man without the power of choice. He would have said, "This is the way; walk in it because you cannot help yourself." He would have *forced* us to love, to serve, to be right. But love would then have been mechanical, and virtue a necessity. God knew better. He desired the spontaneous and voluntary giving of our hearts, or nothing. He wished men to live the truth because they love the truth.

Moreover the history of all forced religion, where the constraint has come from the outside rather than from within, has been that it leads to formalism, hypocrisy, decay, and death.

' So let us not try to force the truth on anyone. Let us give it to them, and when it has been presented in its own fair garment and bodied forth in our lives, men will want it for its own sake. Nor need we fear to wait. The world is hungry for the truth as the thirsty sands for the advancing tide.

Meanwhile if your heart longs to help, lift up your eyes unto the fields, they are white already to 'the harvest. Thousands on thousands are ready for your word. If they will not take it in one city go to another; if not in one home go to another. You do not need to waste your time with those who do not want it when so many are calling for help. All people are your brother and sister and mother. Go ye into all the world and preach the truth to all. Turn to the people nearest you, however, whenever you can. Although a prophet is rarely honored in his own country, yet there is where he should begin. Start where you are, help where you are, if possible. If you are faithful in a few things, you will be made a ruler over many.

If you desire to make the giving of this truth and healing to the world your life work, begin with those about you. Gradually you will find others coming of their own accord to you for help and you will wake some morning to find yourself a successful healer and teacher, a blessing to your day and generation.

LESSON IV.

HOW LONG TO TREAT AND HOW OFTEN.

IT is a mistake to suppose that the value of a treat ment lies in the length of time you hold the thought. As a matter of fact you are working in a timeless element. In mind, whatever is known must be known immediately or not at all. All you have to do is to "register" there. Your ability to do so quickly will depend upon your consciousness. The use of affirmations, denials, treatments, realizations, reading, arguments, and so on is not for the sake of the patient but for your own sake. You must follow such a course as will bring your faith up to the point where *you know* in your heart that the word you speak will heal. It is the experience of all healers that our consciousness is higher at some times than at others. In exalted moments we speak the word and the patient is at once healed, if receptive. At other times it may require closely applied thought and argument to bring our faith up to the required intensity to register in the Creative Mind.

As to how often we should take the patient into the silence, that is also a question of conditions. If he is not readily receptive we must continue to make our advance on chaos and the dark. We must treat until an opening is secured, for while we treat none but those who desire help, yet race prejudices, religious formalism, and such things may prevent the patient from easily receiving. He may be like the New Testament character who exclaims, "Lord, I believe, help Thou mine unbelief." The object of repeated treatment is therefore to be sure that we have made a full realization in consciousness.

Again the thought of some people is easily changed; they vacillate and accept contrary suggestions. I have had patients who could not hold to an idea more than a day or two at a time. In such cases I have found it necessary to give them daily instruction and treatment until the seed of faith had time to root. Do not be discouraged at seeming failure; you do not know when it may turn to brilliant victory. So long as the patient is depending on you, go on daily affirming the truth of being and leave the rest to God.

LESSON V.

WHAT KIND OF CASES TO BE TREATED.

HOW inadequate are words! We do not treat anything, we neither manipulate the disease, the body, the mind of our patient, our own, nor Creative Mind. We simply realize the truth of being and that does the work for us. "Ye shall know the truth and the truth shall make you free" There is no disease in spirit. So-called organic disease has no more reality than functional; functional has no more reality than we give it. Disease is in the thought and is cured by the change of thinking. Some disease thoughts appear to be more firmly rooted in the mind of the patient than others, but remember that all the power there is is to be applied to every case and you will find one class of disease as curable as another. We have known of too many cases of so-called incurables whose ailment melted into nothing, to be mistaken in our conclusion that "with God all things are possible." He who claims otherwise is unacquainted with the principle with which we work. God is the healer, truth is His weapon, and that weapon it is given us to use. Do not hesitate to treat any case to which your consciousness can rise.

At the same time, when you take a case be sure that you feel within yourself a sufficient elevation of con sciousness. If, after meditation, you find you do not have the necessary confidence do not hesitate to sur render the case to another healer. It is more than mental dishonesty to accept as a patient one whom you do not feel able to heal. For example, suppose the case to be total blindness, or deafness, or a broken limb; do you think you will be able to heal it? If so, go on. It has been done, it can be done. But if you know that your consciousness will not rise to this point, then turn away the case. Be honest with yourself and others. Avoid the danger of fakerism. Do not bring this great movement into disrepute by joining the army of mere tax-gatherers. **You Are in This Work for but One Great Purpose—to Heal. Your Business Is Not "Treating Patients" but Healing Them.**

At the same time do not underrate your consciousness. If you feel that with God all things are possible and that you have faith enough to see this patient well or prosperous, then go on, for you cannot fail. God will add to you "the universal plus." "Give, and it shall be given unto you; good measure, pressed down and running over shall be given into your bosom."

Whatever you can conceive of yourself as having or doing, you can do. Have no fear; all error will yield to truth.

SPECIAL REALIZATIONS.

ON LOSS BY DEATH.

"I am the God of Abraham; for God is not the God

of the dead but of the living; for all are alive unto God."

The healer will present the following thought either audibly or silently to the patient:

The first necessity to comfort is to realize that "death" is only the name to an event in life. No one really dies. *Life* cannot be lost. God does not see death at all because He knows only life. (See page 109).

We may liken life, or the spirit of man, to a dove as it is spoken of in the Bible. When the cage in which it is confined is broken up, the dove is set free. It soars away into the sky and out of sight and we say, "I have lost the dove." But we know that somewhere it is alive, somewhere it is free and happy. It has not lost itself and it flies in the sunlight of the same sun that shines on us. The dove is for a time lost to us, but it is not lost to *itself*. As God sees only *life* and all "are alive unto Him," there was no change in the life of the dove when it flew away from the box. So the dove or "spirit" is not lost to itself or to God. It is lost only to our *conscious* mind. We are the only ones who feel the change as loss.

Moreover the spirit has not lost us. Its first instinct as it leaves the body is doubtless to come to those dearest to it and bless them. As it is immaterial, and mind is immaterial, it can communicate its love to our mind. But thought and love are silent and not violent forces. Therefore the soul must be still to receive the still small voice of love. If the waters of our life are troubled, spirit cannot make an impression on it with its gentle breeze of thought.

To agonize and trouble and "sorrow as those who have no hope" is to cut ourselves off from the comforting presence of God and from the love of the dear one flowing back to us.

It is not that we should desire to be told the mysteries of the beyond, "for if one return from the dead we will not believe him," but rather that we should feel the comfort of the spirit's "All's well," as it directs its loving thought to us. It may even cause it distress for it finds us so chaotic in thought and feeling that it can get no response from our deep inner mind—the mind in us that even now can rejoice in the mysteries of the soul.

Sleep and rest are therefore earnestly to be sought, and a peaceful mind; and it is wrong to lose one's poise. Weep? Yes, if you wish, shed tears over the parting that takes place physically. Stoicism is not a vast virtue but your tears are not the violence of fear or regret. Nor would you hold back the onward-pressing soul. It has gone on to other forms of unfoldment and experience. Bless it, and let it pass. Some day for you the silver chord shall break and you too shall pass into the newer and higher land. Meanwhile God keeps His watch-care over you both—the dear one there, you here, just as the same sun shines on your friend in the east while you are in the west, or north, or south

(Compose the mind of your patient, and then take the following realization.)

You are now conscious of the Indwelling God and the God in whom you dwell. You feel that to know Him is life eternal. You know that He is never-ending life and you know that you and your dear one are children of the Father; therefore the life of both is eternal. God knows no death and with Him there is no separation for "all are alive unto God," as Jesus said. You feel peace and quiet and calm. You rest in divine peace and quiet. (Now go on realizing the truth for "Peace," page 214, and, if the patient needs it, for "Sleep," page 215). Exercise deep faith, command the taut strings of mind and body to relax and mentally order sleep to come. When it comes, use the realization of the presence, page 170, and then rest your mind in peace, or quietly leave your patient.

For Nerve Troubles, Headaches, Neurasthenia, Indigestion, Etc.

Nerve troubles are due to reaction from mental pressure of one kind or another. Many people feel hurried in their work even when no hurry is needed; they work under pressure. Others think about one thing too long, constantly dwelling on one thought; "harping on one string," worrying over one thing. A severe shock to the physical system has often turned the attention of the mind to the body and brought on "nervousness." Fear can often be found as the first cause. Many people say "This noise, that person, etc., get on my nerves," and then the sensitive system takes them at their word and they get discordant. Analyze the cause. Try it out before the court of reason. You are out of harmony with your world. You believe that "something is wrong somewhere." Stop thinking that. The way to get things right is to think right. Get into harmony with your world. Nerve trouble is due to inharmony and the way to be rid of it is to come once more into harmony. Make your union with men, environment, and God. If you are not right, get right. Get right mentally. If some one is out of harmony with you and that distresses you, make a statement that they are really at one with you for you both are one at the heart of the universe.

Now take the realization for peace. Hold this truth in mind for a while and say "I am at one with all people and all things. I rest in the sure confidence that beneath me are the girders of the Almighty and underneath are the everlasting arms."

If you need it, realize the truth for sleep. After a while you will feel these truths to be true and they will externalize for you the thing you desire.

Conquering Fear, Doubt and Faultfinding.

"He that overcometh shall inherit all things."

I have the power of truth in me, therefore I will not make mistakes: I have the power of love in me, therefore I shall keep in harmony with all things and people; I have the power of life in me, therefore I shall possess all health, today. I do now overcome all tendency to doubt, to fear, to find fault, to fall into my old mistakes. I am master of my appetites, passions, habits and, above all, my thoughts. I overcome all desire or interest in negative things and thoughts. Therefore Today I do inherit the kingdom of God— the kingdom of love, joy, and peace. Accordingly all things that are good are also mine and I am grateful to God for the beneficent law of life which gives me these things. I thank Thee, Father, for these things. Amen.

Independence and Freedom.

"Where the spirit of the Lord is, there is liberty."

In me is the spirit of the Living God. The life I live is the life of the Spirit; the love I feel and express is the love of the Spirit; the wisdom I show is the wisdom of the Spirit. The Spirit of the Lord is upon me and I feel His presence in and through me. The spirit of the Lord is everywhere and in everything and I cannot get out of it if I would; I would not if I could. Therefore am I at one with It in spirit and in truth. I welcome the thought of God; I meditate upon Thee, and am glad. There is nothing opposed to Thee, for Thou art all. There is nothing outside of Thee; there is no place where Thou art not. Since Thou art perfect freedom, I also am free. Since Thou art the limitless, nothing can bind me. Where nothing binds, there is freedom. Since I am son of God there can be only limitless action for me. I am free. I have liberty. Nothing binds me but love and my own will. I am not hampered by men's opinions or prejudices. I am not hampered by traditions. I am not bound by convocations, creeds or confessions. I am bound only by the rectitude of my own heart. If the opinions and prejudices of men seek to bind me I will throw off the shackles and be free. I will not act thus and so because other men so act, but because I wish to do as I will. If I do not wish, I do not act. My friends would not try to make me act contrary to my own inner feeling: others cannot. I act only on the impulse of my own soul, on my own initiative. I am an independent spirit. I am an independent thinker. I am an independent worshipper. I am my own standard and my own judge. I am conscious of the glorious freedom of a son of God. I am filled with happiness and joy, for I am master of my own fate and I carve out my own destiny. **I Will Be What I Will to Be, by the Help of God. Amen.**

Faith and Trust in Spirit.

"Commit thy ways unto the Lord, trust also in Him and He shall bring it to pass."

I realize that it is not I that do the works but my Father dwelling in me. I realize that my power is not *without* but *within*. That my power is the power of the spirit. That all is spirit and therefore "all power is given unto me in heaven and on earth." I therefore commit my ways unto the one wisdom, and the one power—Spirit. I trust in the inner wisdom and guidance. I trust only in the way of Spirit. I

seek no outside aids to Spirit and spiritual consciousness. The Spirit is creative and makes all things. It
is wisdom and knows how. Therefore I commit my
ways unto It that It may bring to pass. I commit
my ways unto It by my thought since Spirit is Mind
and acts by thought. I therefore perceive my good,
and Spirit takes my thought and works upon it, while
I sleep. I give my desire to Spirit and it goes on
working for me ceaselessly. I wait and trust and
receive. I rest in quiet confidence. My good is coming to me, for God is now on my side and working
on my problem. For this I give thanks.

PEACE AND HEALTH.

"O Lord, my God, I cried unto Thee and Thou hast
healed me."

I now assume toward God an attitude of expectant
faith. I now look to the Law of Life for my deliver
ance. No longer do I depend upon material things but
on the law of my own inner being. Today I make
my unity with good, with God, and with the Law.

I am at one with all the highest and best. I am at
one with the universal laws. I am at one with all men
in highest friendship. I am at peace with my world.
I am free from sense of struggle. I am free from
sense of irritation and fear. I know no friction in
my life and today I refuse to see imperfection anywhere. This is my cry unto God, I have closed my
eyes to the darkness that I may see the light. I have
closed my mind to evil that I may think only good.

I turn my back on poverty that I may perceive my supply. I recognize only the good, the beautiful and the true. Therefore have I cried unto thee, O Lord, and declared my faith in God and Good. Therefore am I sure of my healing. I am indeed made whole, for Thou hast already answered my prayer and because I have refused to recognize evil I have already found that there is nothing for me but good. I give Thee thanks for all things. So be it!

SLEEP.

"When thou liest down thou shalt not be afraid; yea, thou shalt lie down and thy sleep shall be sweet."

I rest in perfect confidence in God. Nothing can come to me but good for God is good and where He is there can be no danger or harm. I do not fear to-day because I trust in the protecting power of Divine Love and Wisdom. I will not indulge my subtle fears or misgivings. I will not allow fearful thoughts to come to me. I have set my mind on high things. It is my will that my mind shall be stayed on the thoughts of faith and peace. Why should I be afraid when Thou keepest me. He that keepeth me neither slumbers nor sleeps. He gives his angels charge over me to keep me while I wake or sleep. Because I have set my love upon Him, He shall deliver me. I will not allow the old worries to vex my mind. I will not allow myself to be disturbed by people or things. I will not be nervous or fearful. I will not because I cannot when my mind is stayed on Thee, O Lord, my

Light and my Salvation. "The Lord is the strength of my life, of whom shall I be afraid?" I am afraid of nothing. I am full of peace. Thou restorest my soul. "Peace I leave with thee, my peace I give unto thee; not as the world giveth, give I unto thee. Let not your heart be troubled, neither let it be afraid." So do I rest in quiet trust and faith all day, and because my mind is at peace all day, it is also at rest and at peace at night. I give thanks for the love and watchful care that Divine Love keeps over me.

PROSPERITY.

"With God all things are possible."

I depend on no less a supply than the Infinite. Here there is no limitation. There are no conditions. There are no qualifications. All things are possible. I am a child of God and share His nature and resources. Therefore all things are possible to me. I accept therefore no less than the best and the most that I need and desire. I do not fear lack or limitation. God can lift me out of all my difficulties, and He does so lift me today. I shall pass through all my present problems into the sure solution through the Divine Wisdom and Supply. I go my way today in perfect peace and satisfaction because Thou art with me and for me. I give Thee thanks, My Father.

FOR THOSE IN TROUBLE.

"He leadeth me beside the still waters."

I rest in a new calm and peace today because He

leadeth me. My troubled soul is still. My fears are gone. The vexing problems of life are forgotten. I am entered into the secret place of the Most High. I am at peace and at rest, today. I go my way with an untroubled spirit. "Thou wilt keep him in perfect peace whose mind is stayed on Thee." The things that have been troubling me are now passed away for I feel the greater interest in the finer things of Spirit. What evil can come to the heart that is at peace with Thee? I fear no evil, for Thou art with me. Yea, though I pass through the valley of the shadow Thou art with me. Eternal life is my portion. The broken threads shall yet be woven together. My problems shall yet find their solution. I shall again see my dear ones. I can wait and I can trust and I can rest in Spirit. This pain, this grief, this problem shall pass away and I shall find my peace. So I find it today, since God is the same yesterday, today and forever. I enter the timeless chambers of my soul. I meet with Spirit. I talk with God. I am in the throne room of Spirit and I am satisfied. Father, into Thy hands I commend my Spirit. There I rest today in quiet peace. Amen.

WISDOM AND ILLUMINATION.

"Then shall thy light break forth as the morning and thine health shall spring forth speedily."

There is a light of understanding within me which is capable of interpreting all things. This light is the Wisdom of God in my own soul. It is God's revela-

tion of Himself to me. I am more and more conscious
of this inner wisdom and its power. Open my eyes,
O God, that newer and greater visions may appear,
that I may ever grow in my capacity to think, act,
and speak only those things that are real and true. My
vision is growing brighter day by day. Therefore I
am led to act more wisely. I am acting more and
more in line with the creative will; therefore I am in
harmony with the laws of the universe and they are in
harmony with me. Accordingly health springs forth
from my inner being. I keep the law and the law
keeps me. Health wells up within me as from hidden
springs. Life fills me to overflowing. Joy thrills
through my soul today, for I have made my at-one-
ment with the life of the Universe, and the Father and
I are one. I give thanks for the unspeakable gift of
spiritual understan 'ing.

PROSPERITY.

"In the days of prosperity, be joyful."

I will not forget to give thanks 'or my prosperity.
Therefore I will give thanks now, for All Supply is
mine now and the wealth of the world is at the
command of my faith. "Before they call, I will
answer them," therefore the good I seek is mine now.
"When ye pray, believe ye have received and ye shall
receive." I believe that in the realm of spirit where
all things first exist as thought, *my good has already
been born and has begun to grow for me.* Therefore
I believe that in the Divine Mind I have already re-

ceived. Accordingly I know that I shall receive in an objective way, since every thought must pass out into form. I can and do give thanks in this confidence. Therefore I am filled with joy now in my prosperity. I am filled with great joy, for I not only have the prosperity I seek, but I have that greater thing—the power to conceive and the power to accept a larger measure of good from the Giver of every good and perfect gift. I rest in divine satisfaction and infinite peace. I render thanks for the light, the life and the supply that are mine.

FORGIVENESS AND HEALING.

"Who forgiveth all thine iniquities, who healeth all thy disease."

Today I am conscious of the forgiving love of Spirit. God is my Father, full of infinite love and tenderness. I therefore know that all my mistakes are not held in Divine Mind. I alone have not forgiven myself. I alone have indulged the negative thought of weakness. God forgives all my mistakes and I will therefore forgive myself. If I have done ill to another, I will right it. I will be square with all men. I will overcome my fault. I will rise above my weakness. Therefore do I now forgive myself. I do not sympathize with myself or my fault, but I shall make it a thing of naught by rising so high in consciousness that this desire or temptation cannot again mar my joy in my own perfect selfhood. Therefore I am free from sense of guilt and fault. I rise to new heights.

I go on in a new and conscious freedom. I am full of joy and peace. Therefore I am made whole and my whole body is full of light and health. I am full of thanksgiving.

GUIDANCE IN AFFAIRS.

I am now entered into the Mind that knows all. In the deep silence of my mind I am in touch with All-Wisdom. Here is where every thought begins. I am conscious that this Mind in me knows just what to do under these circumstances. While I, the objective mind, do not know just how to act yet this mind in me does know and *knows* **now.** I therefore charge you, my inner self, to choose out the best course for me to follow in this enterprise. You will then put it into the form of thought and thought in turn will become the act. I pass from the truth in mind, through the truth in thought, into the truth of right action. I now trust in the inner guidance of spirit. Let all my affairs be made smooth and harmonious. Let all my business arrangements fall into line with prosperity. Let me now act wisely. I now know that the thoughts that come to me along this line will be right and I shall do the right thing at the right time. I may not be conscious at the time that I am acting under the guidance of my intuitions but I will so act. For I am now committing my ways unto the Lord—I am trusting in Him and He shall bring it to pass.

All my affairs shall now go well. My business plans shall carry through. I shall succeed in this enterprise and I shall not lose heart or courage. It is *now* done, *already,* in the Creative Mind. It is accomplished and I am glad to give thanks.

LETTING DOWN.

To relieve the sense of tension and pressure, it is necessary to realize the three-fold basis of feeling.

We perceive

> "Nor soul helps flesh more now
> Than flesh helps soul."

The physical organism needs to be made quiet and reposeful. A good method to follow for those under special tension is to sit or lie down and begin the process of relaxation. Go to each part of your body in turn and give your orders. "Arm, relax! Leg, relax! Muscles of the throat, relax!" You will find that you have been under tension. Perhaps the shoulders or the back will be found bracing up against the weight of care. Or the abdomen has been held in and needs to be unchecked. Whatever it is, it will respond to your will, and even the involuntary muscles and nerves will respond to your orders. Rest and quiet will seize upon you, and you will feel singularly free.

Now you must see to it that the moral feelings are under control. It is impossible to make your unity with the All-Good if you feel yourself to be wrong somewhere, and as this sense of unity is absolutely essential, you must seek to make yourself right in thought and act with others, yourself, and the Infinite

Law of Life. To have "clean hands and a pure heart," and "a conscience devoid of offense to God and man," is to find relief at once. Remember that the Law is not out of harmony with you but only you with it. "Before they call, I will answer them." Therefore forgive yourself for your mistakes, for you are a "son of man" and "the son of man hath power on earth to forgive sins." In treating others, mentally declare that their sins are forgiven and that thus there is no sense of separation from God in their minds. Jesus seems invariably to have forgiven sin before healing. "Son, thy sins are forgiven thee, now rise, take up thy bed and walk."

Next you must unlimber the mind. It will be a surprise to you to find how much you have been worrying. You have been afraid of your work or the opinion of others. You have feared failure. You have wanted too much. Your mind has been at tension all the time. Day and night your tired brain has gone on toiling, puzzling, anticipating. You find it hard to give this all up. But it can be done. There are many ways. First of all, there is the determination to change, to have a new set of interests and stick to them. Conversion means a change of mind and the reason why religious experience, which we call a re-birth, is of value, is that the whole course of thought is changed. The interests of life are altered. The old is found discordant, the new attractive. Turn your mind to consider what wonderful things growth and self-development are. "Desire earnestly the better things."

Forget your old worries and problems by engaging in new interests. Learn to take more concern for others. This will help. Get away from yourself. You are too important—to yourself! You do not bulk so large as you think! Be more modest. You are not Atlas carrying the world on your shoulders. Carry on a little argument with yourself. "My work is getting on all right. I will forget it now. I will thus feel fresher for it tomorrow. Better things are coming. It will come out all right. The future has many wonderful things in store. Life is good. I am enjoying my rest or recreation now. I feel no resentment against anyone. I fear nothing nor anyone. I am carefree. I am bound to be happy—now."

Burdens will slip the mind. Care will fly away as it should. A sense of lightness and of warmth will pervade the mind.

Unleash the hounds of fear and worry and haste and let them go! Rather the simple, happy life of moderate circumstances than the warped and twisted threads of an unhappy and unhealthy life!

* * * * * * * * * *

Thus may the seeker for truth become the Great Finder, for he who seeks shall find; he who knocks at the portal of Wisdom shall have it opened unto him, and this shall be the nature of his marvelous discovery:—**"I and the Father Are One."** To know that Spirit passes through **us** into expression, that creative energy is a servant waiting the command of thought, and that we are the thinkers of that thought, is to give us a sense of power and mastery. The master key to life is Unity. All the ills of life are due to inharmony, inharmony is due to a sense of separation and lack of unity. But when we have once more made our unity with All-Good we become bond servants no more to the Law, but rather the Law becomes our servant while we pass into the glorious freedom of the sons of God. Receive therefore the Spirit of truth, rise to the conscious union wherein you may say, "I and the Father are one" and enter your kingdom in the conscious recognition of the "Christ in You, the hope of glory."

MY GOOD-NIGHT PRAYER

Now let me sleep. In peace I lay me down
　　As draws the day to close:
Good day or ill, no more it vexes thought
　　Than when at morn I rose.

Now on the breast of night once more I lie
　　As when a child I lay
Close in the warm embrace of mother-love,
　　Worn with the hours of play.

I rest and breathe a prayer to God tonight
　　And feel His presence near,
Whose power is great, Whose wings o'er-
　　shadow me
And guard my heart from fear.

Dark though the night, I closer press to God
　　He sees beyond the dark
And knows the good that yonder lies for me—
　　He hears the morning lark.

So let me sink to rest in dreamless sleep—
　　Flee, cares, to shadows dim!—
My soul shall find its peace in God and wake
　　From sleep to joy in Him.

F. L. H.

Made in the USA
Las Vegas, NV
21 June 2022